People of the Ancient World

ANCIENT INDIA

WRITTEN BY
VIRGINIA SCHOMP

Franklin Watts
A Division of Scholastic Inc.
New York Toronto London Auckland Sydney
Mexico City New Delhi Hong Kong
Danbury, Connecticut

Note to readers: Definitions for words in bold can be found in the Glossary at the back of this book.

"So free am I, so gloriously free" by Mutta (page 84) was translated by Uma Chakravarti and Kumkum Roy.

Photographs ©2005: akg-Images, London: 59 (Paul Almasy), 20, 23, 30, 38, 82, 86, - (Jean-Louis Nou); Art Resource, NY: 25, 28 (Erich Lessing/British Museum, London, Great Britain), 43 (Erich Lessing/Musee des Arts Asiatiques-Guimet, Paris, France), 13 (Prince of Wales Museum, Bombay, Maharashtra, India), 29, 94 left (Scala/Government Museum and National Art Gallery, Madura, Tamil Nadu, India); Bridgeman Art Library International Ltd., London/New York: 4 center, 89 (Ancient Art and Architecture Collection Ltd.), 24, 94 right (Giraudon/National Museum of India, New Dehli), 46 (National Museum of Karachi, Pakistan), 69, 95 top; Corbis Images: 15 (Archivo Inconografico, S.A.), 77 (Bettmann), 49, 70 (Burstein Collection), 32, 40, 78, 81 (Lindsay Hebberd), 85 (Historical Picture Archive), 68 (Angelo Hornak), 90 (Sanjib Mukherjee/Reuters), 63 (Galen Rowell), 42 (Stapleton Collection), 19 (Gian Berto Vanni), 44, 52, 54; Dinodia Picture Agency/T.S. Satyen: 41; Harappa.com/J.M. Kenoyer, Courtesy Dept. of Archaeology and Museums, Government of Pakistan: 62; Hulton|Archive/Getty Images: 93 right, 96; Los Angeles County Museum of Art, (c) Museum Associates: 71 (Anonymous gift, M.87.272.8, *Adorant with Garland*, 1st century B.C., Pakistan, Swat Valley, Gandhara region), 37, 95 bottom (Gift of Mr. & Mrs. Subhash Kapoor, M.85.72.1, *Elephant with Riders*, 3rd-2nd century B.C., India, Uttar Pradesh, Mathura), 48 (Gift of Dorothy and Richard Sherwood and Mr. & Mrs. Harry Lenart, M.77.15, *The Sati of Ramabai, Wife of Madhavrao Peshwa*, c.1772-1775, India, Maharashtra, Pune); National Geographic Image Collection: 51 (Christopher Klein), 9 (Randy Olson); Peter Langer Associated Media Group: 31, 55; The Art Archive/Picture Desk: 73 (National Museum Karachi/Dagli Orti); The Image Works/The British Museum/HIP: 26, 27, 92, 99; Woodfin Camp & Associates: 60 (Jehangir Gazdar); www.art-and-archaeology.com/Michael D. Gunther: 75.

Cover art by Rene Milot
Map by XNR Productions Inc.

Library of Congress Cataloging-in-Publication Data

Schomp, Virginia.
    Ancient India / Virginia Schomp.— 1st ed.
        p. cm. — (People of the ancient world)
Includes bibliographical references and index.
ISBN 0-531-12379-0 (lib. bdg.)   0-531-16846-8 (pbk.)
1. India—Civilization—To 1200—Juvenile literature. I. Title. II. Series.

DS425.S2653 2005
934—dc22

                                                    2004025156

Contents

Introduction   FORGOTTEN GLORIES.............................5

Chapter I   BRAHMAN PRIESTS.............................11

Chapter II   KINGS, QUEENS, AND PRINCES 22

Chapter III   GOVERNMENT LEADERS AND WARRIORS 34

Chapter IV   FARMERS AND MERCHANTS....................50

Chapter V   SERVANTS, LABORERS, AND CRAFTSPEOPLE.....65

Chapter VI   OUTCASTES AND SLAVES......................77

Chapter VII   POETS AND PLAYWRIGHTS 82

Chapter VIII   THE LEGACY OF ANCIENT INDIA 89

TIME LINE 92

BIOGRAPHICAL DICTIONARY...................96

GLOSSARY....................................100

TO FIND OUT MORE..........................104

INDEX...107

FORGOTTEN GLORIES

HISTORIANS HAVE LONG BEEN FASCINATED by the pyramids of ancient Egypt and the splendid palaces and libraries of ancient Mesopotamia. Until recently, they believed that civilization did not develop in India until thousands of years after the start of those two great societies. Then, in the 1920s, **archaeologists** began exploring the Indus Valley region of northwest India (present-day Pakistan). They excavated the ruins of huge cities dating back to about 2700 B.C., around the same time period as early Egypt and Mesopotamia. Their discoveries proved that India had one of the oldest and most advanced civilizations of the ancient world.

The Indus Valley civilization extended over a vast territory that included parts of today's India, Pakistan, and Afghanistan. Farmers raised crops and livestock in the fertile plains of the Indus River and other waterways. Artisans created beautiful pottery, jewelry, and stone and metal sculptures. Merchants traded with faraway lands. They marked their goods with square stone seals carved with images and a type of writing that has never been **deciphered.** The Indus Valley people also built large walled cities, including Mohenjo-daro and Harappa. These cities had straight paved streets, well-built brick houses, and a sophisticated system of private baths and sewers.

Around 1700 B.C., the Indus Valley civilization ended. No one really knows why. Some historians believe that earthquakes and other natural forces caused major rivers to change course, flooding some areas and drying up others. Cities and villages were abandoned. Many people moved eastward, toward the fertile valley of the Ganges River. Around the same time, groups of warlike Central Asian **nomads** known as Aryans crossed the Himalayan Mountains and settled in northern India. Gradually, a new civilization emerged, dominated by the Aryans' language and beliefs.

There is little archaeological evidence showing how India's Aryan people lived. However, they did leave behind two major collections of literature. The *Mahabharata* and the *Ramayana* were **epic** poems telling exciting stories of wars, kings, and heroes. The **Vedas** were books of religious poems, hymns, and rituals that became the first scriptures of **Hinduism.** The period of Indian history from about 1700 to 500 B.C. is called the Vedic Period after these sacred texts.

By the end of the Vedic Period, India was divided into sixteen major states and kingdoms. Under a ruler named Bimbisara, the land of Magadha in the Ganges Valley became the largest and most powerful state. Around 322 B.C., Chandragupta Maurya seized the throne of Magadha. This bold war leader conquered and united the divided kingdoms of northern and central India, founding the Mauryan Empire.

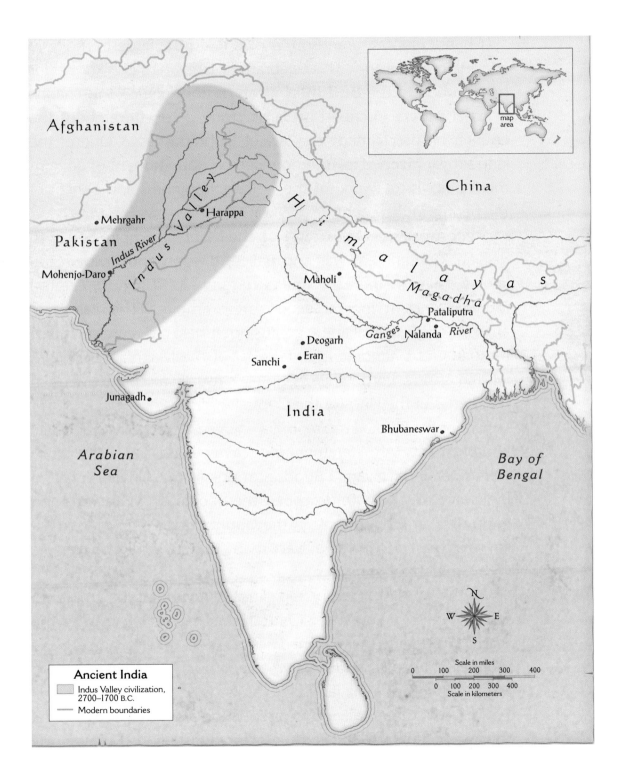

Afghanistan

China

Pakistan

• Mehrgahr

Harappa •

Indus River

Indus Valley

Himalayas

Mohenjo-Daro •

Maholi •

Magadha

Pataliputra •

Ganges   River

Nalanda •

Deogarh •

Sanchi •   • Eran

Junagadh •

India

Bhubaneswar •

Arabian
Sea

Bay of
Bengal

map
area

N

W   E

S

Scale in miles
0   100   200   300   400

0   100 200 300 400
Scale in kilometers

Ancient India

Indus Valley civilization,
2700–1700 B.C.

——— Modern boundaries

Chandragupta's grandson, Asoka, ruled the largest empire in ancient Indian history. This celebrated Mauryan ruler is known for his devotion to the **Buddhist** ideals of nonviolence and charity. In royal **edicts** inscribed on large stone pillars throughout the empire, he proclaimed "the law of Righteousness." One of the king's royal **inscriptions** announced his appointment of government officials to "work for the welfare, happiness and benefit of the people in the country."

After Asoka's death in 232 B.C., the Mauryan Empire began to decline. Centuries of war and peace, division and invasion followed. Then, in the early fourth century A.D., Chandra Gupta I founded ancient India's second great empire. (The names of ancient India's kings can be confusing! It helps to remember that the name of Chandragupta, founder of the Mauryan Empire, is written as one word, while "Gupta" is usually a separate word in the names of the kings of the Gupta Empire.)

Under the Gupta Empire, India enjoyed a golden age of peace and prosperity. Art, literature, and science flourished. All religions were tolerated. Faxian, a Buddhist monk from China who visited India around A.D. 400, described the people as "numerous and happy." Even though most of the Gupta kings were Hindus, Faxian was pleased to observe "very many [Buddhist] **monasteries,** with a multitude of monks."

By the late fifth century, rebellions had divided the empire. A series of invasions by fierce Central Asian warriors known as the White Huns further weakened Gupta rule. India's golden age gradually dwindled and died. In the centuries that followed, the glories of ancient India faded into legends or were forgotten.

Today, historians rely on a combination of written and physical sources to uncover the facts behind the legends. They study ancient Indian texts, including the Vedas, the great epic poems,

Local workers help archaeologists uncover a site dating back to the ancient Indus Valley civilization.

and Buddhist chronicles. They read royal inscriptions and ancient accounts by foreign visitors. Archaeologists look for evidence beneath India's sun-baked deserts and fertile river plains. Using tools that range from picks and shovels to the latest computer technology, they explore the remains of ancient cities, villages, workshops, and temples. By analyzing and comparing all these sources, they have pieced together a portrait of Indian life through the ages.

There is still much work to be done. Historians continue to search for clues to unravel the remaining mysteries of India's ancient civilizations. Their work helps us understand the many ways these brilliant societies influenced later civilizations in Asia and around the world. Through their explorations of ancient India's culture and accomplishments, we learn how the past has shaped our modern world.

Chapter I

BRAHMAN PRIESTS

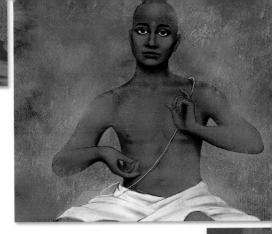

To learn how the people of ancient India lived, we must first take a look at their religious traditions. Religion was the foundation of Indian society. It affected work, play, marriage, family, education, the arts, and nearly every other aspect of daily life.

Ancient India was the birthplace of several major religions, including **Jainism** and Buddhism. However, the faith that played the most important role in shaping Indian society was Hinduism. In fact, some historians have called this complex combination of beliefs and practices the "essence of India."

The Growth of Hinduism

Hinduism was born out of a blending of the religious beliefs of the Indus Valley civilization and India's Aryan settlers. The early Hindus believed in a host of gods associated with the sun, the moon, wind, fire, and other natural forces. They worshipped their gods with animal sacrifices. The **Brahmans,** or priests, who performed these complicated rituals recited sacred hymns that had been memorized and passed down for generations. Sometime after 1500 B.C., they began to write down their hymns and ritual formulas. Out of those writings came the four sacred texts known as the Vedas.

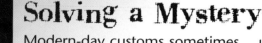

Solving a Mystery

Modern-day customs sometimes help archaeologists solve mysteries of the past. In 1982, a team of Indian and American archaeologists excavated a ten-thousand-year-old settlement in central India. They found the remains of a small stone platform. At the center was an unusual triangular stone, engraved with a series of smaller and smaller triangles. At first, the scientists could not figure out the meaning of the ancient stone. Then, not far from the site, they came across a newly built platform topped with six similar stones. A local villager explained that the painted stones represented the Mother Goddess. Like their ancestors centuries earlier, Hindus still came to the platform to worship the goddess and ask for her guidance and protection.

By the sixth century B.C., India's ancient faith had become a stale collection of rules and rituals that few people besides the Brahmans could understand. A number of reformers emerged to challenge the authority of the priests. New religions such as Buddhism offered fresh ideas that made sense to ordinary people.

The Brahman priests responded to these challenges by absorbing many of the teachings of the rival faiths. Gradually, Hinduism developed into a strong, flexible religion uniting people of all backgrounds and beliefs. By the time India entered the golden age of the Gupta Empire, this enduring faith had developed essential principles that continue to this day.

Enduring Beliefs

One of the basic principles of Hinduism is **reincarnation.** Hindus believe that each person has an eternal soul, which is reincarnated, or reborn, in a new body after death. The form of rebirth

Brahman, the One God, is shown in the center of a stone sculpture from the Gupta Empire.

depends on the individual's **karma.** Karma is the sum of all the good and bad actions performed by the person during past lives. According to the Upanishads, a set of ancient commentaries on the Vedas, a man might be reborn "as a worm, or as a butterfly, or as a fish, or as a lion, . . . or as a person, or as some other being in this or that condition, according to his works."

To achieve a better rebirth, an individual must live according to his or her **dharma.** Dharma is the set of specific religious and social duties divinely assigned to each person according to his or her place in society. Those who fulfill their dharma may eventually achieve **_moksha,_** or liberation. In this state of perfect knowledge and happiness, individuals escape the cycle of death and rebirth and merge with Brahman, the One God. The Upanishads describe Brahman as

> That from which beings are born,
> that by which, when born, they live,
> that into which, when dying, they enter.

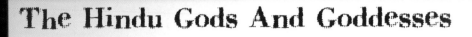

The Hindu Gods And Goddesses

The ancient Hindus worshipped thousands of gods and goddesses, which were all believed to be different forms of Brahman, the One God. Here are a few of the best-known deities, with some of their special (often overlapping) characteristics.

Brahma the Creator	Created the universe and set it in motion. Brahma is traditionally shown with four heads, each reciting one of the Vedas. He is the first of the three gods of the Hindu Trinity (along with Vishnu and Shiva).
Vishnu the Preserver	The Preserver of the Universe. Whenever humankind needs help, Vishnu appears on Earth as an avatar (reincarnation). He is traditionally shown as dark blue, with four arms, often riding on the mythical bird Garuda.
Shiva the Destroyer	God of both destruction and creation. His destructive powers remove the world's impurities. He rides the sacred white bull Nandi.
Mother Goddess	God in the form of the Divine Mother, Great Goddess, or Mother Goddess. She embodies pure love and creative energy. All the Hindu goddesses were considered forms of the one great Mother Goddess.
Parvati	Goddess who is the consort, or wife, of Shiva. Her many forms include the golden goddess Uma, the angry ten-armed Durga, and the bloodthirsty Kali.
Lakshmi	Consort of Vishnu and goddess of wealth, fertility, and good fortune.
Sarasvati	Consort of Brahma and goddess of music, literature, and wisdom.
Rama	The sixth avatar of Vishnu. As the hero of the epic *Ramayana,* he defeated the world's most powerful demon, Ravana.
Krishna	The seventh and most important avatar of Vishnu. He delivered the sermons of the *Bhagavad Gita.*
Ganesh	Elephant-headed son of Shiva and Parvati. One of the most beloved gods, he is wise, thoughtful, and jolly.
Indra	God of battle and chief administrator of Heaven.
Surya	God of the sun who was widely worshipped in early Vedic times.
Agni	God of fire.
Varuna	God of rain.
Yama	God of death.

Because the One God can take many different forms, there are thousands of Hindu gods and goddesses. Most of the people of ancient India devoted themselves to one of the three most popular deities. Vishnu was the Preserver of the Universe. Shiva was the god of destruction and rebirth. A Mother Goddess embodying love and creative energy was called by a number of different names. In Gupta times, passionate devotion to a chosen god became one of the most popular paths to spiritual liberation.

One way Hindus show their devotion to their gods is through a ritual known as **puja.** During a puja ceremony, the worshipper lavishes care on a sacred image believed to contain the god's spirit. The statue is bathed, dressed, offered gifts of food and flowers, and entertained with music and dancing. Archaeologists have found many sacred images of gods and goddesses in ancient Hindu temples.

The Caste System

The organization of Indian society was rooted in Hindu beliefs. According to the Vedas, India's Aryan people were loosely divided into classes, based on their wealth, power, and occupation. Over time, those divisions grew increasingly rigid. The Hindu principles of reincarnation and karma led to the idea that people were born into a particular class because of how they had lived in past lives. Each class had its own divinely determined dharma. Those who fulfilled their dharma by faithfully following the

The Hindu Mother Goddess can take many different forms. She often represents love, fertility, and creation.

The Divine Origin of Castes

A hymn from the *Rig-Veda,* the most ancient Vedic text, explains that the caste system was created when the gods divided the first man into parts.

What did his mouth become? What his arms?
What are his legs called? What his feet?
His mouth became the brahmin;
his arms became the warrior-prince,
his legs the common man who plies his trade.
The lowly serf was born from his feet.

laws and customs of their group could hope for rebirth in a higher class.

The Indians called their system of social classes **varnas.** European observers used the word **castes.** There were four main castes. At the top were the Brahmans, or priests. Next came the **Kshatriyas,** who were traditionally rulers and warriors. Beneath these upper classes were the **Vaishyas,** who included farmers and merchants. The lowest caste were the **Sudras,** who were mostly servants, laborers, and craft workers. At the very bottom of society were people with no caste at all, known as **untouchables.**

Within the four main classes, there were thousands of *jatis,* or subgroups. The jatis were based mainly on family descent and hereditary occupation. For example, a Sudra might be born into the barber jati. His father and grandfather were barbers, and he most likely would follow the same trade. However, even if he never worked as a barber, he would remain in the barber jati all his life. So would his children and their children, down through the generations. Westerners often use the word "caste" for both the four main classes and the many smaller subgroups.

All castes were ranked according to the spiritual purity of their work and way of life. A priest's occupation was considered far more pure than a barber's. A caste whose members were vegetarians had a higher status than groups that the sacred laws permitted to eat meat or fish.

The Sacred Laws

Around A.D. 200, Hindu priests compiled the *Laws of Manu,* a collection of "the sacred laws of each of the varna." This ancient text spelled out hundreds of different rules concerning nearly every aspect of daily life. The most important rules related to work, marriage, and food. Hindus were expected to work in one of their caste's traditional occupations and to marry someone from their

A Brahman's Diet

The sacred laws included many dietary do's and don'ts for each of the castes. These rules were especially strict for Brahmans. According to the *Laws of Manu,* members of the highest class should not eat food derived from animals, except meat sacrificed as part of a religious rite. They should avoid food served by anyone who was sick, angry, or drunk. Also forbidden was food "touched intentionally with the foot, . . . pecked at by birds or touched by a dog, . . . food at which a cow has smelt, . . . that on which anybody has sneezed," and food served at a dinner "where a guest rises prematurely and sips water."

own class. Complex rules determined what kinds of foods people of each caste could eat and who could prepare, serve, and share their meals.

In reality, the Indian way of life was never as rigid as the ideal system outlined by the priests. People often worked in nontraditional jobs. They sometimes married outside their caste, and another complex set of laws governed the status of children of these "mixed marriages." Also, at some times and places, membership in a trade guild or a powerful family was considered just as important as a person's caste. Despite these variations, all Indians accepted the basic rules of the class system and tried to live up to their religious and social duties.

A Privileged Class

According to the *Laws of Manu,* the Brahman was "the lord of all castes." His sacred duties were "teaching, studying [the Vedas], sacrificing for himself, sacrificing for others, making gifts and receiving them."

All members of the top three classes had the right to study the Vedas, but only a Brahman could teach those holy texts. Priests also had the exclusive right to perform sacrifices and other religious ceremonies on behalf of other people. The sacred nature of their work brought great respect, along with a number of privileges. These benefits included the right to live on gifts donated by members of the other classes. According to the sacred texts, people who gave to the Brahmans earned rewards in their next life. Those who gave land were especially blessed, because they would be "liberated from all sin." Such promises ensured that priests received generous gifts of land and other valuables, sometimes even entire villages. As an added benefit, no matter how wealthy Brahmans might become, they did not have to pay taxes.

A stone relief (a sculpture that stands out from a flat background) shows a Brahman teacher. Only Brahmans were permitted to teach the sacred texts known as the Vedas.

Hindu Temples

The first Hindu temples were built out of wood. None of these ancient sanctuaries has survived. In Gupta times, the Indians built hundreds of Hindu shrines and temples out of stone. While most of these buildings were later destroyed by foreign invaders, a few are still standing.

One of the finest Gupta temples is at Deogarh in northern India. Built in the sixth century A.D., this stone monument is dedicated to the god Vishnu. Carvings of scenes from Hindu mythology cover the doorway and walls. One wall panel shows the god resting on a monstrous snake. According to a popular myth, the world was created when Vishnu awoke from his long sleep on the "mighty coils [of a] giant cobra" floating on "a vast dark ocean."

Vishnu sleeps on the coils of a snake at the Hindu temple in Deogarh.

Many Brahmans strived to live up to the high calling of their caste. Some served at the royal court, advising the king, tutoring his children, and performing state ceremonies. Some taught in city universities or worked as village priests and schoolmasters. Brahmans often joined religious colonies, devoting their lives to study, meditation, and good works. Others withdrew to hermitages. The holy men of these forest retreats lived in humble bamboo huts, dressed in rags, and survived on one small meal a day. Freed from all worldly cares and desires, they often attracted small groups of followers who came to benefit from their wisdom.

Not all Brahmans were hermits, teachers, or priests. The religious laws permitted members of each caste to work outside their ideal occupations "in times of distress," when they could not earn a living any other way. Ancient texts mention Brahmans working as army commanders, tax collectors, doctors, actors, and even professional spies.

Buddhist accounts also describe corrupt Brahmans who made their living preying on the fears and superstitions of the common people. Traveling through the countryside, these swindlers used "magic" derived from the sacred texts to cast spells and tell fortunes. While some of these tales may be true, others were probably invented or exaggerated by Buddhist critics of the powerful Brahman caste.

Chapter II

KINGS, QUEENS, AND PRINCES

Ancient India's second caste, the Kshatriyas, included government leaders and professional warriors. The king usually came from this class. As the supreme Kshatriya, he was ruler of the kingdom and commander of the military forces.

The people of ancient India believed that their kings were predestined, or divinely chosen, to rule. The king's existence maintained order in the universe. When rebellions and other troubles led to the fall of a king, the natural result was chaos. "A rulerless country is like the waterless rivers," said the epic poem *Ramayana.* "If a king is not there in the world, with his discrimination between good and evil, this world will be dark."

Most of what we know about India's kings comes from written sources. These include ancient Indian texts on government as well as royal inscriptions (pronouncements by kings that were engraved on stone and other hard surfaces). Other good sources are the accounts by foreign visitors to the royal court. Archaeologists have also discovered the ruins of royal palaces and ancient paintings of the Indian court.

Royal Responsibilities

Around the early fourth century B.C., Kautilya, chief minister to Chandragupta Maurya, wrote the *Arthasastra*. This political handbook examined every aspect of good government, beginning with the duties of the king. A ruler's first duty was to serve his people, wrote Kautilya. "In the happiness of his subjects lies a king's happiness, in the welfare of his subjects, his welfare. A king's good is not that which pleases him, but that which pleases his subjects."

India's rulers served their subjects by protecting the land from invasion and maintaining alliances with neighboring kingdoms. Just as important was their duty to preserve the social and economic order. They issued decrees making sure that the laws laid down in the sacred texts were observed. They punished violators of those sacred laws. They developed irrigation systems, promoted trade and business, built and repaired roads, and provided relief to the needy. The king's responsibilities also included observing religious rituals and supporting priests and temples. According to the *Rig-Veda,* a ruler who kept a Brahman priest "well attended, and praises and honors him as a **deity**" would "overpower all opposing forces."

This ancient stone sculpture depicts a "priest king" from the Indus Valley civilization.

Constant Devotion

The *Arthasastra* outlined a strict daily schedule that would allow kings to fulfill all their sacred duties. The timetable gave the ruler

The Horse Sacrifice

Ancient India's most important royal ritual was the horse sacrifice. A fine horse was blessed by the priests and set free to roam outside the king's domain, accompanied by a band of warriors. The chieftains of every territory that the horse entered had a choice. They could fight the soldiers or agree to submit to the king's authority. After a year, the horse was returned to the capital. It was sacrificed to the gods in an elaborate ritual involving hundreds of priests. The ritual was believed to assure power and prosperity to the kingdom. Archaeologists have found gold coins minted by Samudra Gupta commemorating this solemn ceremony. One coin was inscribed, "After conquering the earth the Great king of Kings with the strength of an invincible hero is going to conquer the heavens."

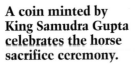

A coin minted by King Samudra Gupta celebrates the horse sacrifice ceremony.

about seven hours out of every twenty-four hours for sleep, meals, and recreation. He was supposed to devote the rest of his time to "constant activity in the cause of his people." He must hear petitions from subjects, meet with government officials and the royal priests, and review the army. The king also had to receive daily reports from the spies who served as his eyes and ears throughout the kingdom.

Historians believe that few kings ever lived according to this high ideal. In fact, some ancient texts poke fun at the superhuman exertions recommended in the *Arthasastra.* However, other sources show that the best rulers did take their duties seriously. The Greek historian Megasthenes, who served as ambassador to the court of Chandragupta Maurya, wrote that the king attended to public affairs "for the whole day without allowing the business to be interrupted." According to another ancient observer, Chandragupta met with government officials "even when [he] is having his hair combed and dressed."

A second-century A.D. sculpture shows the king in his role as divine ruler, chosen by the gods to protect the people. He is surrounded by his attendants, and his hands are raised in a gesture of worship.

King Asoka recorded his devotion to duty in his royal inscriptions. In one edict, the king announced that he had "made arrangements that officials may have access to me and may report on the affairs of my peoples at all times and in all places—when I am eating, when I am in . . . my inner apartments, . . . when I am walking or engaged in religious exercises."

Buddhist Principles

Although all Indian kings lived according to the rites and traditions of Hinduism, many rulers were also devout supporters of Buddhism.

The founder of Buddhism was the Indian prince Siddhartha Gautama, also known as the Buddha, or "Enlightened One." In the sixth century B.C., this great philosopher wandered across India sharing his teachings and founding monasteries. The Buddha taught that all unhappiness was caused by desire. Desire could be eliminated by following the Eightfold Noble Path of right understanding, right thought, right speech, right action, right livelihood, right moral effort, right mindfulness, and right concentration. The path would bring virtuous followers to a state of **enlightenment** and endless bliss called nirvana.

Buddhism included a strong set of moral guidelines. The Buddha encouraged people to "feel all-embracing love to all living beings" and never to lie, steal, or "desire evil for another." Buddhists rejected the caste system. "No one is an outcaste by birth, nor is anyone a Brahman by birth," said the Buddha. "It is by deeds that a person becomes a Brahman." The new faith also rejected the complex rituals and sacrifices of the Brahman priests. While the priests insisted that no one could achieve salvation without their help, the Buddhist path was open to all.

Prince Siddhartha, the future Buddha, leaves home in search of enlightenment.

The Ashes of the Buddha

After the Buddha's death around 483 B.C., his body was cremated (burned) and his ashes were distributed to several different **stupas,** or memorial shrines. In the 1960s, archaeologist Sooryakant Narasinh Chowdhary discovered one of those resting places. Chowdhary was a graduate student at an Indian university. When he found two ancient mounds in a remote area of western India, he began digging. In time, Chowdhary and a team of archaeologists uncovered the remains of an ancient Buddhist shrine. At its center was a round stone box. In the box was a tiny gold bottle filled with ashes. The exciting discovery was confirmed by an inscription reading, "This is the abode of the relics of Dashabala [another name for the Buddha]."

A priest divides the ashes of the Buddha into eight parts, so that stupas all across India can share the holy remains.

Many of India's kings no doubt were sincere converts to Buddhism. Adopting the new faith also helped free them from the authority of the priests and the tremendous expense involved in the complex Brahman sacrifices. Even Hindu kings often included Buddhists among their advisers at court and made generous donations to Buddhist temples, universities, and monasteries.

This stone relief depicts the enlightenment of the Buddha. At the base of the empty throne, the wise man's footprints appear, along with the "Wheel of Law" set in motion by his first sermon.

India's greatest Buddhist king was Asoka. Early in his reign, this powerful Mauryan monarch led a brutal military campaign that killed or wounded hundreds of thousands of people. Overcome by regret, Asoka dedicated the rest of his life to promoting the Buddhist ideals of nonviolence and compassion. In one of his royal inscriptions, the king urged his subjects "to practice charity to all living beings, . . . to tell the truth, observe purity of thought, honesty, . . . to avoid cruelty, spite, anger, pride and envy; to endeavor to do good works, . . . to practice tolerance and respect for other religions."

The Splendors of the Court

Along with its many responsibilities, the role of king also brought tremendous honor and privilege. The kings of the Mauryan and Gupta empires lived in sprawling palaces, surrounded by every luxury. Most splendid of all was the royal palace in the Mauryan capital at Pataliputra (present-day Patna).

According to Greek observers, the palace at Pataliputra was like a small city. Walls, watchtowers, and moats surrounded a vast complex of buildings and courtyards. The outer sector of the palace was open to the public. It included the audience hall, where the king listened to petitions from his subjects, and the almshouses, where he distributed alms, or charitable gifts, to the needy. The grounds also held a music hall, a library, gardens, ponds, and a zoo.

The palace's inner sector held the royal treasury, the **arsenal,** and government meeting halls. There was a vast park with beautiful gardens and artificial lakes stocked with "fish of enormous size, but quite tame." At the center of the gardens were the grand pavilions where the king and his family lived. These magnificent wood and stone buildings were "decorated with gilded pillars and winding golden vines on which silver birds perched."

Hundreds of officials and attendants were needed to run this extensive establishment. The king's personal attendants included a bodyguard of female archers. A host of servants prepared his daily baths, massaged him with perfumed ointments, and dressed him in finely perfumed clothes. Special servants were in charge of the royal umbrella, fan, drinking goblet, shoes, and other essentials. The chief cook personally prepared all the king's meals. These were tested for poison by several food tasters. Dancers, musicians, acrobats, magicians, sword swallowers, and snake charmers provided entertainment.

Archaeologists have uncovered large sections of the ruins of Pataliputra. Their excavations show that the grand Mauryan palace covered at least 4 square miles (10 square kilometers). The buildings were destroyed by fire sometime in the fourth century A.D., and few traces remain of their former glory.

A host of servants hovered about the king, tending to his every need.

The Royal Harem

Most of ancient India's kings had a number of wives. However, only one woman was recognized as the legitimate wife and queen. The others were **concubines,** or secondary wives.

The king's wives and daughters lived in the **harem.** This was a special secluded section for women at the center of the palace. The harem was enclosed by high walls and guarded by a company of female warriors. No man was permitted to enter except the king and one elderly guardian. In literature and sculptures, the guardian was often portrayed as a comical figure, leaning on a cane and grumbling about his many responsibilities.

The women of the harem devoted most of their time to an elaborate beauty routine. This included baths, massages, and expert applications of ointments and perfumes. Each woman had a maid who styled her hair, applied her makeup, and adorned her body with painted designs. Other pastimes included playing games, listening to music, and strolling through the harem gardens. The highlight of the day was the king's visit. Although all the women of the harem accepted the queen's authority, each tried to attract the king's attention with her charm and beauty.

A king relaxes in his royal harem. His wives and daughters lived in this isolated, luxurious section of the palace.

Harem Beauty Supplies

The "makeup kit" of a lady of the Indian royal harem included a wide assortment of paints, powders, and ointments. Each day, servants rubbed her body with a fragrant paste made from a sandalwood tree. They used small sticks to apply a dark eyeliner known as kohl. They painted her lips with an orange-colored powder. They drew decorative designs on her face, arms, shoulders, and breasts with black, white, or red dye. Even the soles of her feet were painted, so that she left a trail of red footprints wherever she walked. The final touch was a dark beauty spot carefully dotted on her forehead.

A lady of the royal court uses a stick to rim her eyes with the dark perfumed paste called kohl.

The Crown Prince

Naturally, most kings had many children. However, only the sons of the queen were eligible for the throne. Kingship generally passed to the ruler's oldest son, known as the **crown prince.**

The prince grew up in a special section of the palace, attended by a host of priests, teachers, and servants. Daily rituals guarded him from evil. Strict studies prepared him for his sacred duties. His education began at age three and included lessons in history, religion, economics, politics, and warfare. At the end of his training,

A wall painting from a Buddhist cave temple shows an Indian prince. Servants are bathing the young ruler as part of a religious ceremony.

he was sent to take part in a military campaign. After he had proved himself in battle, the king might appoint him governor of a province.

Finally, the time would come for the crowning of the new king. First, the royal **astrologers** studied the stars to choose a lucky day for the ceremony. Then a golden pavilion was built at the palace. The pavilion held a sacred fire and piles of jewels and other riches from the royal treasury. In this splendid setting, priests performed solemn rituals confirming the ruler's divine rights and powers.

After the ceremony came the royal procession. Mounted on an elephant adorned with silver and gold, the young monarch rode through the capital, accompanied by a parade of musicians and finely dressed nobles. The *Ramayana* describes a royal procession through streets decorated in "gold and glittering garment." The roar of the crowds "shook the city's tower and temple [as] women with their loving greetings, children with their joyous cry, tottering age and lisping infant hailed the righteous chief and high."

Chapter III

GOVERNMENT LEADERS AND WARRIORS

While the king was the supreme member of India's second caste, the Kshatriyas also included a host of other people. They were the nobles of ancient Indian society, with special rights and duties. According to the *Laws of Manu,* the main duties of the Kshatriya caste were "to protect the people, to bestow gifts [on Brahmans], to offer sacrifices" and "to study [the Vedas]."

As the protectors of the people, the Kshatriyas were in charge of the government and the army. A nobleman might become a general or a high-ranking government official. However, there are also records of Kshatriyas who worked as merchants and artisans. Even when nobles worked outside their traditional occupations, they still enjoyed the privileges of their caste.

The Council of Ministers

The most powerful government officials belonged to the council of ministers. This small but influential group was responsible for setting government policy. According to the *Arthasastra,* the council's role was "to propose projects, to bring works undertaken to a successful conclusion, to examine new possibilities, to maintain discipline in the administration."

The king had to consult his council before making any important decisions. If the ministers disagreed with his policies, they had the authority to criticize or even overrule him. A royal inscription on a pillar in Junagadh in northwest India records one such disagreement. Around A.D. 150, King Rudradaman decided to "increase his religious merit and fame" by repairing a broken dam. His council of ministers decided that the task was "futile [hopeless] on account of the enormous extent of the breach." Deprived of government funds, Rudradaman spent "a vast amount of money from his own treasury and in not too long a time made the dam three times as strong."

Civil Servants and Spies

Government policies were carried out by thousands of officials organized in a vast and complicated **bureaucracy.** In Mauryan times, the kingdom was divided into several large provinces, each governed by a member of the royal family. The provinces were divided into districts. These were administered by deputies appointed by the provincial governor, along with a council of prominent residents. Districts were further divided into cities, small towns, and villages, administered by chiefs and councils.

In addition to these local authorities, the bureaucracy included thousands of other major and minor officials. These civil servants collected tolls and taxes, supervised road construction and maintenance, counted the population, measured the land, regulated water use, and policed the streets. Government magistrates, who might come from the Brahman or Kshatriya caste, judged most legal cases. The penalty for crime was usually a fine. However, a man convicted of murdering a close relative, stealing the king's

The Little Clay Cart

A play called *The Little Clay Cart,* believed to have been written around A.D. 400, gives a lively account of the Indian justice system. In this popular drama, three government magistrates try the case of an innocent man accused of murdering his lover. They interrogate a number of witnesses, including the wily criminal who has falsely accused the virtuous hero. A group of sculptures excavated in Maholi in northern India depict scenes from *The Little Clay Cart.* One image shows the dramatic moment in the last act when the murdered woman is reborn and reunited with the hero.

elephants, or forcing his way into the king's harem could be put to death.

Government officials also kept an eye on business operations throughout the kingdom. They managed government-owned farms, mines, spinning mills, metal workshops, and weapons factories. They kept an eye on all private enterprises. These ranged from stores and factories to houses of gambling and prostitution. Constant supervision ensured that all businesses followed the government regulations covering wages, working conditions, and the quality, quantity, and price of goods.

A special category of government officials were the overseers, or spies. According to the Greek historian Megasthenes, the job of these secret agents was "to enquire into and superintend all that goes on in India, and make reports secretly to the king." Spies watched for signs of disloyalty, dishonesty, and unrest, both within and outside the government. They brought regular reports from their assigned territories to the capital. One ancient poem described the arrival of a spy at court, "his legs tired and heavy with the long journey, . . . his tunic girt up [fastened] tightly by a mud-stained strip of cloth."

The wages paid to government officials varied according to their rank. The *Arthasastra* recommended a salary of 48,000 **panas** (silver coins) for the prime minister, 12,000 *panas* for a provincial governor, and up to 1,000 *panas* for a spy. The government also paid an allowance to the families of civil servants who were injured or had died on the job.

Three fighting men ride a war elephant into battle. One soldier is guiding the animal, while the others prepare to fight the enemy.

Born to Fight

The goal of the kings of ancient India was not only to preserve the kingdom but also to extend it through conquests. To fulfill that ambition, rulers maintained a large standing (permanent) army. According to Greek writers, the army of Chandragupta Maurya numbered more than 600,000 men.

The Kshatriyas were the backbone of the army. Their military education made them the most skillful soldiers, and they held most of the leadership posts. However, ancient texts show that men of other classes also took part in war. Brahmans might become generals, while the lower classes often served as lower-ranking foot soldiers.

Traditionally, the Indian army was divided into four sections, the elephants, cavalry, chariots, and infantry. The war elephants marched at the front of the army, smashing through enemy ranks like modern-day tanks. Each elephant carried a driver and two or three soldiers armed with bows and spears.

Scenes of War

In 1851, British archaeologist Sir Alexander Cunningham excavated ancient India's most impressive Buddhist temple, the Great Stupa at Sanchi. Sculptors from the first century B.C. decorated this massive shrine with scenes from the life of the Buddha. One gate is covered with dramatic images of war. An army of archers, cavalry, chariots, and war elephants attacks the walls of a city. A soldier holding a long shield hurls a spear. A porter at the gate of the fortress prepares to fire one back. Historians believe that the images depict the siege of the ancient city of Kusinagara in southern India. According to Buddhist chronicles, the conflict took place after the death of the Buddha, when rival kings fought over his ashes.

Elaborately carved images of war decorate a gateway at the Great Stupa of Sanchi.

The cavalry was used for surprise attacks and other situations requiring speed. Some historians believe that the effectiveness of the cavalry was impaired by an unusual custom. Before battle, the horses were given a large drink of wine.

India's war chariots were made of wood covered with metal plates. Early chariots were small, light, and swift. Over time, however, chariots became increasingly large, heavy, and difficult to maneuver. In 327 B.C., Alexander the Great invaded India and battled a force of war chariots that one ancient Roman historian described as "scarcely of any service." Each of the bulky chariots was "drawn by four horses and carried six men. . . . The chariots kept sticking in the [mud] and proved almost immovable from their great weight."

The infantry was the largest division of the Indian army. It was responsible for most of the fighting on the open battlefield and in **sieges.** According to another Roman observer, foot soldiers carried "a bow made of equal length with the man who bears it," which fired arrows "little short of being three yards [3 meters] long." Ancient Indian sculptures show infantry soldiers armed with these long bows as well as swords, spears, battle-axes, and daggers.

The Four Stages of Life

Just as Indian society was divided into four great classes, so life was divided into four stages. These four ideal stages were student, householder, hermit, and wanderer. The stages were reserved for the men of the three upper classes. Few Indians ever completed them exactly as outlined in the sacred texts. However, all men accepted the stages as a worthy framework for living, and many tried to follow the ideal path.

Student life began with initiation. This **sacrament** signaled a boy's spiritual birth and made him a full member of Hindu society. A Brahman boy was initiated at age eight, a Kshatriya at age eleven, and a Vaishya at age twelve. During the initiation ceremony, the boy received the "sacred thread." This woven cord was draped over one shoulder, across the chest, and under the opposite arm. The boy would wear his sacred thread for the rest

The sacred thread, a symbol of the Hindu faith, can be seen on this statue of the god Shiva. The thread indicates a young man's spiritual birth.

of his life, as a sign that he was "twice born," once through his physical birth and once through his spiritual birth.

Following initiation, a Brahman or Kshatriya boy traditionally went to live in the home of a **guru,** or spiritual teacher. There he studied the Vedas, learning thousands of verses from the sacred texts by heart. Kshatriya boys were taught the skills of archery, swordsmanship, and hand-to-hand combat. They practiced one of the earliest forms of martial arts, a fighting style that combined wrestling, throws, and deadly hand strikes. Many gurus also gave lessons in grammar, literature, painting, music, dancing, math, and science.

Some boys studied in a Buddhist monastery school instead of the home of a guru. The most famous Buddhist school was founded in Gupta times at Nalanda (present-day Bihar). According to the Chinese Buddhist monk Faxian, the teachers at Nalanda gave lessons in grammar, medicine, Hindu philosophy, and Buddhist principles. At its height, the school had a student body of ten thousand young men.

A Kshatriya boy usually concluded his studies sometime after age sixteen. At that point, he was expected to return home and marry a girl who had been chosen by his parents. Marriage made the young man a householder. One of the most important duties of the householder was to produce sons. Only a son could carry on the family line and perform the sacred rituals that honored the family's ancestors. If a nobleman's wife did not produce a son, he

Science and Math

By Gupta times, India's sciences were highly developed. Doctors were able to diagnose and treat a variety of illnesses. They operated on the brain and the eyes, and they performed plastic surgery to reattach severed ears and noses. The Indians also made remarkable advances in **astronomy.** In A.D. 499, the astronomer Aryabhata observed that the world was round, that it rotated on its axis, and that it revolved around the sun.

Some of ancient India's greatest advances were made in the field of mathematics. About 2,200 years ago, the Indians developed a counting system based on nine digits and a zero. Later, the Arabs adopted this system and passed it on the West. The numbers, known as Arabic numerals, became the basis of the counting system used today all over the world.

Today, many Indian boys still study the Vedas with gurus. In ancient times, these honored teachers also gave lessons in science, math, medicine, and other subjects.

A painting from a later century depicts an Indian marriage ceremony in ancient times. The marriage would have been arranged by the parents of the young man and woman.

might bring one or two concubines into the household. These secondary wives usually came from a lower caste.

The Three Aims

A householder was expected to devote himself to the three traditional aims of life. The first of these objectives was righteousness, which meant following the sacred laws. As part of his sacred obligations, the householder performed a variety of rituals at different times throughout the day. Most important were the offerings made before the fire that was kept constantly burning in every home's hearth. The entire family assembled by the fire for these rituals. Family ties were extremely important to the Indians.

A Kshatriya's family might include not only the married couple and their children but also the husband's uncles, aunts, nephews, nieces, cousins, and other close relatives.

A householder's second most important objective was wealth. A poor man could not possibly perform all his religious duties and ensure his family's happiness. The god Vishnu was often held up as an example of the ideal combination of wealth and virtue. The Preserver of the Universe lived amid great luxury in his heavenly court, with Lakshmi, the goddess of wealth, by his side. Yet he was all-merciful, rushing to Earth whenever the weak and unfortunate needed his help.

The third aim of life was pleasure. While this was the least important of the three objectives, it seems to have played a major role in the lives of many Kshatriyas. The pleasures of a nobleman's life included painting, literature, drama, dancing, and music. Nearly every cultured man and woman owned a **vina,** a small harplike instrument played with a bow. The Indians also played flutes and other reed instruments as well as a variety of drums,

A group of people play instruments in a stone relief from a stupa. The figure on the far right is playing a vina.

An Ancient Game

A favorite pastime of young Indian nobles was the military strategy game **chaturanga.** A text written around A.D. 620 described the pieces used in this popular board game. The pieces included the king, the elephant, the horse, the chariot, and four pawns representing the four divisions of the army. In time, *chaturanga* would spread throughout the world. Today, we know it as the game of chess.

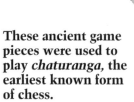

These ancient game pieces were used to play *chaturanga,* the earliest known form of chess.

gongs, cymbals, and bells. Among the householder's other amusements were social gatherings, board games, archery contests, gambling, and animal fights.

The *Kamasutra,* or "Rules of Love," written sometime before the seventh century A.D., offered the well-to-do young householder detailed instructions on the art of fine living. The book advised the nobleman to pay careful attention to his appearance, bathing and applying "a limited quantity of ointments and perfumes to his body" each morning. His daily round of pleasures might include conversing with friends, going on picnics, teaching his pet parrots to speak, and "holding festivals in honor of different deities." Evenings were the time for singing, playing with dice, and "similar other amusements." After that, the householder "should await in his room, previously decorated and perfumed, the arrival of the woman that may be attached to him." Only by balancing his religious duties and his pursuit of wealth with pleasure could a man enjoy "happiness both in this world and in the world to come."

The Final Stages

According to the *Laws of Manu,* a householder who saw "his skin wrinkled, and his hair white, and the sons of his sons" was free to enter the third stage of life. Leaving his home, he could retire to a hermitage. In this forest retreat, the hermit spent his days studying the scriptures and performing rituals. He also practiced yoga. Followers of yoga performed difficult postures and other forms of physical and mental self-discipline. Their goal was to achieve spiritual enlightenment and the liberation of the soul. Archaeologists have found evidence of this ancient discipline as far back as the stone seals of the Indus Valley civilization.

In his old age, a truly devoted man might end his days as a wanderer, the fourth stage of life. The seventh-century A.D. chronicle *Harsacarita,* or the "Deeds of Harsa," described a wanderer with a shrunken face and eyes "as red as drops of wine." Dressed in a tattered rag, the holy man carried his few possessions on a cord, which was slung over his back. Freed from all worldly desires, he wandered the land, begging for his daily

A stone seal from the Indus Valley civilization shows a man in a yoga position.

meals. Wanderers were greatly respected for their spiritual purity and wisdom.

Worthy Wives

While Kshatriya boys studied with their guru, their sisters often were educated at home by a tutor. A girl's studies might include literature, painting, singing, dancing, and other arts. From her

On the Menu

The people of India's upper classes ate a varied diet. Depending on the religious restrictions of their caste, their meals might include rice, beans, boiled or fried wheat and barley, fruits, vegetables, and fish. A wide variety of meats completed the menu. Among these were boiled, fried, or roasted goat, deer, tortoise, parrot, porcupine, and alligator. A favorite dish was roasted peacock wrapped in bitter leaves, served with a mango-and-butter sauce. Most dishes were highly seasoned with **curry,** cinnamon, ginger, and other spices. After a flavorful feast, wealthy nobles enjoyed an assortment of desserts, including fresh fruit, flavored milk **curds,** and spicy rice balls rolled in sugar.

mother, she learned the skills of cooking, weaving, embroidery, and managing servants. The goal of her education was to prepare her to fulfill the sacred duties of a wife and mother.

Most girls were married by the time they turned sixteen. A wife was expected to devote herself to ensuring her husband's comfort and happiness. She spent most of her time at home, managing the household and caring for the children. Even if the family had many servants, she prepared and served her husband's meals personally, in accordance with the religious rules.

The *Arthasastra* listed a variety of punishments for wives who neglected their duties. A wife guilty of "going out at daytime to sports" paid a fine of six *panas* to her husband. The penalty for going out "while the husband is asleep or intoxicated" was twelve panas. Women who carried on "secret conversation" with men "in suspicious places" could be whipped "five times on each of the sides of their body."

A Widow's Sacrifice

The ancient Indians traditionally cremated (burned) the bodies of the dead. Beginning in the sixth century A.D., some Kshatriya widows chose to join their husbands on the funeral **pyre.** The self-sacrifice of a **sati,** or "true wife," was considered the ultimate demonstration of a woman's devotion to her husband. A small, engraved pillar in Eran, India, records the first known sati. Erected in A.D. 510, the stone records the death of the chieftain Goparaja in battle. It also honors his wife for sacrificing herself on his blazing pyre.

An approving crowd celebrates the self-sacrifice of a widow on her husband's funeral pyre.

A Kshatriya wife treated her husband with great respect and tried to fulfill all his needs.

Despite all the restrictions, well-to-do Kshatriya women often enjoyed considerable honor and influence. A wife had complete authority over all household affairs. The personal goods that she brought into her marriage remained her property, and she could pass them on to her daughters. Sacred texts heaped praise on the "worthy wife" and commanded husbands to treat their wives with gentleness and respect. "Women must be honored and adorned by their fathers, brothers, husbands, and brothers-in-law," said the *Laws of Manu.* "Where women are honored, there the gods are pleased, but where they are not honored, no sacred rite yields rewards."

Chapter IV

FARMERS AND MERCHANTS

India's third caste was the Vaishyas. According to the *Laws of Manu,* the duties of this class were "to tend cattle, to bestow gifts [on Brahmans], to offer sacrifices, to study [the Vedas], to trade, to lend money, and to cultivate land."

In early Vedic times, nearly all Vaishyas were farmers. By the age of India's great empires, some members of this class had built their small landholdings into large estates. Other Vaishyas worked as merchants or traders, often specializing in a particular type of goods such as spices or perfumes. No matter how wealthy and respected a Vaishya landlord or trader might become, he was still considered inferior to a Brahman or Kshatriya. As one of the burdens of his caste, he had to pay higher taxes than any of the other classes.

On the Farm

The great majority of Indians were peasant farmers. Most farms were small, providing barely enough to support a single family. There were also a few great estates, worked by large forces of hired laborers. While some farm estates were privately owned, most belonged to the king or the temples.

India's most important crop was rice. Farmers also grew wheat, barley, sugarcane, sesame, cotton, and a variety of

An imaginative modern illustration takes us inside a merchants' shop of the Indus Valley period. In this scene, traders have brought the merchant beads, turquoise, and other fine goods.

fruits and vegetables, including mangoes, peas, beans, lentils, and gourds. The most common farm animals were cattle, buffalo, and sheep. A single cowherd or shepherd often watched over the herds for an entire village.

Ancient Indian texts and accounts by foreign visitors describe the sophisticated methods farmers used to get the most out of their land. Crops were rotated and fields were fallowed (left unplanted for a season) to keep the soil fertile. Manure and other animal and plant products were used as fertilizer. Different plants were sown at different times of the year. That allowed farmers to harvest a variety of crops from spring to winter.

A clay figure from the Indus Valley city of Mohenjo-Daro shows oxen pulling a farmer's or merchant's cart.

From early times, farmers used irrigation to bring water to their crops during India's long dry season, which usually stretches from October to May. Irrigation systems included deep wells, reservoirs, and canals equipped with pumps and other devices to control the flow of water. The Greek historian Megasthenes described "sluices [gates] by which water is let out from the main canals into other branches so that everyone may have an equal supply of it."

Kings often demonstrated their concern for their subjects by overseeing extensive irrigation projects. The government also supported agriculture by lending seeds, farm tools, cattle, and money to farmers breaking new ground. The *Arthasastra* directed the government officials in charge of agriculture to make certain that the work of farmers "shall not suffer on account of any want in plows and other necessary implements."

Village Life

Most of the people of ancient India lived in farming villages. Early villages were surrounded by a wall or fence to keep out wild elephants, lions, and tigers. Inside the village walls, homes might be clustered around a central well or laid out in districts.

Most villagers lived in simple one-story homes. A typical dwelling had mud walls, a dirt floor, and a thatched roof of grass, reeds, or palm leaves. There was little furniture, usually just a wooden bed and tray stands made of rattan (woven palms). The family sat on the floor. They ate their simple meals off large banana leaves instead of plates. Their diet consisted mainly of boiled or fried rice, vegetables, and sometimes meat or fish flavored with spices. For drinking, there was water, milk, or a milk product called **whey.**

An Ancient Settlement

Archaeologists exploring the Indus Valley region have discovered evidence of one of the earliest known farming settlements. The settlement of Mehrgarh dates back to around 7000 B.C. Excavators have uncovered villages of mud-brick huts, along with pottery and other remains. Impressions of grains show that the people of Mehrgarh raised wheat and barley. They stored their crops in large rectangular granaries.

In the deepest, oldest levels of the settlement, archaeologists found the bones of wild animals, including swamp deer, wild goats, and wild pigs. Later levels contained the bones of **domesticated** sheep, goats, and cattle. Those discoveries show that the people of Mehrgarh switched from hunting to animal farming around 6000 B.C., more than three thousand years before the start of the Indus Valley civilization.

This photograph provides a bird's-eye view of the excavated settlement at Mehrgarh.

A man and woman tend to farm chores, including gathering supplies and caring for the livestock.

Village life followed the rhythm of the seasons. From early spring to winter, the men plowed, planted, tended the growing crops, and brought in the harvests. Women managed the household, cared for the children, and pitched in when extra hands were needed in the fields. Older children worked alongside their parents. After celebrating their initiation, Vaishya boys usually studied the Vedas at village schools.

Religion was an important part of village life, with its own seasonal celebrations. At specific times throughout the year, families performed rituals to ensure the gods' blessings on the household, crops, and livestock. The entire village took part in joyous festivals honoring the gods and spirits. During one fall festival celebrating the birth of Krishna, young men climbed on one another's shoulders, trying to break pots of butter and curds hanging over the streets. The game recalled an ancient tale of shepherds who greeted the god's birth by "sprinkling and smearing each other with curds, milk, water, and cream."

Festivals must have been a welcome break from the many hardships plaguing the life of the peasant farmer. Severe droughts and floods could destroy crops. Earthquakes and tornadoes could wipe out an entire village. Added to these natural disasters was the burden of taxes. Vaishya farmers paid a yearly tax equal to one-quarter or more of their harvest. They also paid their share of a general tax on the village, along with many special taxes for government services such as land surveying and canal repairs.

In order to pay their taxes and support their families, peasants often had to borrow money from wealthier landowners. If a farmer could not repay his debts, he might lose his land and all his possessions. Then he would have to earn his living as a paid laborer. Even worse, according to ancient beliefs, the debtor would become the lender's slave in his next life.

Country and City Merchants

Ancient India had five principal types of merchants. The milkman sold fresh curds. The oil merchant sold food oils, which he extracted from seeds with the press at the back of his shop. The spice seller filled his stall with jars, pots, bags, and boxes holding cinnamon, ginger, mace, basil, and other flavorful herbs and spices. Perfumers offered a wide variety of perfumes, powders, pastes, extracts, incense, and other products for scenting the

Fashion Parade

The basic garment worn by men and women of all classes in ancient India was the **dhoti.** This was a length of plain unstitched cloth wrapped around the lower body and tied at the waist. It could hang like a skirt, or it could be pulled through the legs to make a kind of short pants. A peasant might wear little more than a simple dhoti and a **turban** on his head. Upper-class men might top their dhoti with a longer skirtlike garment and a fine shawl.

Peasant women often dressed in a simple skirtlike dhoti and blouse. Women of the upper classes might wear an elaborately draped and pleated gown or a **sari.** The sari was made from a length of cloth wound around the body to cover the wearer from neck to toe. The fine fabrics favored by wealthy women were brightly dyed. Their robes were often decorated with embroidery and glittering ornaments of gold, silver, and gems.

home and body. The tavern keeper sold alcoholic drinks. His work was profitable but not entirely respectable. Tavern customers often included pickpockets, robbers, con artists, and other criminals. Fights were common, and the owner had to be tough enough to toss troublesome clients into the street.

In large towns, merchants clustered together in market districts. Ancient paintings show that these crowded neighborhoods looked a lot like modern-day Indian markets. The cobblestone streets were lined with small shops. The open front of each store was closed at night with wooden shutters. The merchant and his family lived in a house behind the shop.

While a poor city dweller's home looked much like a peasant farmer's hut, wealthy merchants lived in considerable luxury. The house of a rich merchant or noble was usually several stories high. Windows and balconies on the back wall of the house overlooked a private courtyard. In this peaceful haven from the noisy city, the family relaxed amid flower and vegetable gardens, ornamental pools, and pavilions for games and entertaining. Every elegant home also had a bathhouse. This stone or brick building was like a modern-day spa. It held a swimming pool and a steam room with stone benches set around a central fireplace.

In the Market District

The streets of a city's market district bustled with activity. Simply dressed peasants mingled with richly adorned nobles riding in curtained litters carried by porters. Deliverymen and servants hurried on errands. Housewives carried their purchases in baskets hung from an arm or balanced on the head. Jugglers, snake charmers, and monkey trainers performed on the street corners.

Shoppers could choose from a colorful assortment of merchandise. Besides the goods in the merchants' stores, there were handicrafts on display outside artisans' workshops. Farmers from the surrounding countryside sold fresh vegetables, fruits, and other produce, brought to market in heavy ox-drawn wagons. Food stalls offered cooked rice, vegetables, chunks of meat, and other ready-to-eat snacks. Peddlers wandered the streets, selling a variety of trinkets. In ancient paintings and sculptures, peddlers are often shown carrying their goods in two sacks, which dangle from the ends of a carrying pole balanced over their shoulders.

The government kept a close eye on all buying and selling. Officials periodically inspected the scales that merchants used to weigh out orders. They made sure that sellers paid their taxes and

These ruins were once a bustling market in the Indus Valley city of Harappa. The outlines of some of the merchants' stalls can still be seen.

followed all the rules regulating the quality and prices of merchandise. Government spies mingled with tavern customers, watching for signs of drunkenness and dishonesty. According to the *Arthasastra,* drinkers who were "found to possess gold and other articles not their own" would be arrested. So would those who were "too extravagant or spend beyond their income."

These weights and scales were used by Indian merchants in ancient times.

From the Mint

Most customers in ancient Indian markets paid for their purchases with coins. Archaeologists have found thousands of ancient gold and silver coins in a variety of shapes and sizes. Many early silver coins bear several punch marks. These impressions were made by government authorities to verify that the coins were legal. The markings include figures of the sun, trees, peacocks, dogs, elephants, lions, horses, and other images. According to ancient texts, a coin expert could tell where and when a coin had been minted by reading its punch marks. However, the key to the markings has been lost, so modern-day historians can only guess at their meaning.

Trade Routes and Caravans

Many merchants made their fortunes in international trade. By the beginning of the Mauryan Empire, India had well-established trade links with China, the Middle East, East Africa, Greece, and Rome. Indian merchants imported and exported goods along a vast trading network that included both land and sea routes. Foreign trading ships also called at the great port cities that dotted the entire Indian coast.

The Indians exported a wide variety of goods. These included spices, salt, ivory, gold, pearls, fine woods, fabrics, dyes, perfumes, incense, cosmetics, buffalo and rhinoceros horns, tortoiseshell, birds, and animals. In return, traders mainly imported luxury items such as fine pottery, silver and bronze vessels, glassware, and horses.

The taxes, tolls, and other fees paid by traders were an important source of government income. To keep that money flowing,

Exporting Buddhism

Wherever India's traders went, Buddhism traveled with them. From its beginnings in the sixth century B.C., the religion drew most of its followers from the Vaishya caste. Prosperous merchants and traders, who were considered inferior to the two higher classes, were attracted to Buddhism's message of social equality. They carried Buddhist beliefs and art along the trade routes to Central Asia, Southeast Asia, and China. From China, the faith spread to Korea, Japan, Tibet, and other lands. In the ninth century A.D., Buddhism began to die out in India, but elsewhere it was on its way to becoming a major world religion.

the kings sent embassies east and west, advertising India's wares. One embassy set sail to Rome in 25 B.C. with an exotic cargo including snakes, tortoises, pheasants, and tigers.

Kings also built and maintained river ferries and roads throughout the kingdom. The Greek historian Megasthenes reported that India's excellent roads featured signposts at intersections, distance markers at regular intervals, and rest houses offering water and shelter. The government also encouraged trade through policies protecting traveling merchants from theft.

One side of an ancient molded terra-cotta tablet depicts a boat that could have been used by Indian traders for importing and exporting goods.

According to the *Arthasastra,* local officials were required to reimburse any traders who were robbed while passing through their town or village.

Despite these safeguards, trading journeys could be very dangerous. Gangs of fierce bandits roamed the forests. Travelers along desert trade routes risked death from thirst, hunger, quicksand, and wild animals. For protection, traveling merchants usually banded together in trade **caravans.**

A caravan often included hundreds of people. An experienced guide organized the expedition and led the way. Caravans passing

Merchants may have traveled in trade caravans along this rough path, which was part of the Silk Road. That ancient trade route crossed India on its way from China to the Western world.

A Long-Lost Ship

In June 2003, farmers in a southern Indian village dug up a surprise. The men were plowing a rice field when they noticed the planks of a ship sticking out of the ground. Soon archaeologists came to investigate. Using scientific dating methods, they determined that the sailing vessel was about 920 years old. It was made out of local wood, but the building techniques were not Indian. The archaeologists concluded that the shipbuilders must have come from China, Japan, or Egypt or another Arab country. By the twelfth century, India had longstanding trade links with all these lands. The ship probably sank off the coast during a trading voyage. Over the centuries, the coastline shifted as new land built up, creating the inland farm field.

through jungles traveled by day. During desert crossings, caravans traveled in the cool of the night, while a "land pilot" plotted the course by the stars. The travelers carried jars and bottles filled with water, which was strictly rationed throughout the journey.

An ancient collection of Buddhist tales known as the Jatakas contains many stories of desert crossings. In one tale, a caravan's land pilot falls asleep, and the oxen pulling the wagons plod in the wrong direction all night. The next morning, the travelers run out of water and "lay down grieving." Then the leader saves the day by locating a small clump of grass. Digging a deep well beneath the plant, the thirsty men uncover "a new spring in the hot-sand desert."

Chapter V

SERVANTS, LABORERS, AND CRAFTSPEOPLE

The fourth and last caste in Indian society was the Sudras. The people of the Sudra class were considered far inferior to Brahmans, Kshatriyas, and Vaishyas.

While the higher castes were "twice born," Sudras had "one birth only." They had no right to the initiation ceremony that marked a boy's spiritual birth and made him a full member of society. They were forbidden to study the Vedas. One religious law declared that any Sudra who listened to Vedic verses should have molten lead poured in his ears.

The Sudras were permitted to study some of the other sacred texts of Hinduism and to take part in private religious rituals. They were also entitled to some protection under the law. However, their legal rights were limited by the small value placed on their lives. According to the *Laws of Manu,* a Brahman who murdered a Sudra could purify himself by giving another Brahman "ten white cows and one bull." That was the same penalty he would pay for killing a cat, dog, or frog.

Second-Class Citizens

According to Hindu beliefs, the Sudras were born into their lowly caste because of evil deeds committed in their past lives. The only way they could overcome their bad karma was to faithfully fulfill the sacred duties of their caste. A Sudra's most important duty was to serve. "The service of Brahmans alone is declared an excellent occupation for a Sudra," said the *Laws of Manu.* A man who could not find work with a Brahman could support himself by serving a Kshatriya or a wealthy Vaishya. He could also "maintain himself by handicrafts."

There is little written or archaeological information on the lives of ancient India's lower classes. Historians believe that some Sudras became low-level civil servants, clerks, or merchants. However, most of these "second-class citizens" worked as servants, laborers, or craftspeople.

Servants and laborers were usually attached to wealthy landowning families. They worked in exchange for food, lodging, and wages. Under the religious laws, they were supposed to eat the scraps from their master's table and wear his worn-out clothes. The laws also provided wage earners with some protections. Employers had to draw up contracts specifying their workers' hours, duties, and wages. They had to provide employees with the tools they needed to do their jobs. If a master violated the terms of a contract or dismissed a worker without just cause, he could be prosecuted.

Sudras were also required to work in the government labor force for one or two days a month. They might be assigned to a textile mill or a weapons factory. They might work on a large agricultural estate, processing rice, flour, or sugar. Besides the Sudras, the workers in these state-owned enterprises included convicted criminals, widows, orphans, and women of all classes who had

Dating Ancient Artifacts

Archaeologists have found iron nails and arrowheads in India dating back more than 2,300 years. How do they figure out the age of such ancient artifacts? One of their most accurate methods is **carbon dating.**

Carbon dating was developed in 1949 by American physicist Willard Libby. The science is based on the fact that all living things contain a type of atom called carbon 14, which slowly decays after death. Archaeologists know how much carbon 14 an object such as an ancient bone or shell would have had while living. They also know how quickly the atoms would have decayed. By measuring the remaining carbon 14, they can tell how long ago the object died. Many iron artifacts can be carbon-dated because they contain charcoal, which comes from plant or animal sources.

been deserted by their husbands. Royal decrees protected the modesty of upper-class women who were forced to work for a living. They were allowed to do their weaving at home and bring it to the shop before the workday began. Superintendents were forbidden to look them in the face or speak to them about anything but their work. Officials who broke any of these rules paid fines ranging from forty-eight to ninety *panas.*

A Variety of Crafts

The artisans of ancient India worked in both small villages and large cities. Most were independent tradesmen. Some craft workers were employed by large enterprises where goods were made on an "assembly line," with each worker responsible for one step of the process. Trades were nearly always hereditary and were

Ancient India's blacksmiths made a wide variety of objects from metal. These copper spearheads date back to the Indus Valley civilization.

practiced by the entire family. Often groups of families following the same trade lived together in the same village. A village on the outskirts of a city might be entirely populated by blacksmiths, potters, or weavers.

The Indians were highly skilled in a variety of crafts. The most important village craftsman was the carpenter. Carpenters built wooden buildings, boats, wagons, beds, storage chests, and many other useful items. Before chopping down a tree, the carpenter always made an offering to the spirit living within it, asking release from "the blame for dislodging him."

Another essential trade was blacksmithing. Smiths worked with iron, copper, tin, and other metals. They turned out essential objects including shovels, axes, saws, hammers, nails, knives, spears, needles, and cooking pots. The Iron Pillar of Delhi is a famous example of the skill of ancient India's ironworkers. Erected in honor of Chandra Gupta II, the huge pillar was made from a single piece of solid iron. Although it has stood in the sun and rain for more than 1,500 years, it shows almost no signs of rust.

The Iron Pillar of Delhi was made from a solid piece of iron weighing more than six and a half tons. A protective layer of iron and other elements has kept the pillar nearly rust-free for centuries.

A potter from the Indus Valley civilization made this jar from clay and decorated it with paintings of birds and other designs.

Potters made clay pots and jars. They gathered clay from the shores of a lake or river. They mixed it with water and other materials and molded it on a potter's wheel, which was turned with the foot. Pottery was baked in shallow trenches between layers of smoldering wood. The hardened vessels often were decorated with simple painted or engraved designs.

Indian basket makers wove a wide variety of household objects, including baskets, trays, boxes, brooms, umbrellas, and matting for roofs and floor coverings. Most basket makers were women. They worked with reeds, grasses, bamboo, and other plant materials.

Women also worked with textiles. They spun thread and wove cloth from wool, cotton, hemp, flax, and some types of grass and bark. The finished products ranged from tough tent cloth to silky cotton for a wealthy noblewoman's skirts. Dyers colored the cloth with vegetable and mineral dyes. Embroiderers decorated fine fabrics with gold and silver thread.

Another important Indian craft was garland making. Artisans skilled in this craft arranged cut flowers, feathers, berries, and other ornaments in a variety of beautiful garlands. Wealthy men and women wore fresh flower garlands every day. The strands were also used as religious offerings and street decorations during festivals.

Trade Guilds

In very early times, Indian artisans began to organize in professional groups known as **srenis,** or "guilds." Historians have found records of about thirty different trade guilds, including ones for carpenters, smiths, potters, painters, ivory sculptors, jewelers, and merchants. There also may have been guilds of professional beggars and thieves.

A master craftsman known as the elder served as the head of each guild. This powerful official usually

The man depicted in this ancient sculpture is holding a flower garland. Garland making was one of ancient India's most honored crafts.

Ranking by Craft

Trade guilds were an important subdivision of Indian society within the larger division of castes. Ancient stories and inscriptions often describe individuals by their profession instead of their class. The social status of the different trades varied, depending on the purity of the work. Carpenters had a relatively high status because they assisted the priests in religious rituals performed before the building of a new house. Shoemakers were despised because they worked with the hides of dead animals.

inherited his post, although there are some records of guild elections. The elders of important guilds often took part in government assemblies. Some even served as counselors to the king.

An elder's responsibilities included setting standards for the quality of manufactured goods and issuing rules regarding wages and working conditions for workers in craft factories. He also met with the leaders of other guilds to set prices for raw materials and finished products. Kings and government officials recognized and enforced the regulations laid down by the guilds.

Trade guilds often acted as banks for their members, lending money and accepting deposits. They served as courts of law, judging disputes between members and punishing those who violated guild rules. Many guilds maintained their own private armies to safeguard caravans and trading posts. In wartime, these militias fought as part of the royal army.

Over time, some guilds built up considerable wealth and influence. The richest guilds functioned as charitable institutions, helping the needy and building shrines. In the first century A.D., a guild of ivory workers donated one of the four massive carved gateways of the Great Stupa at Sanchi. Centuries later, a guild of silk weavers built its own impressive Hindu temple.

The World of Art

Many Indian artisans ventured beyond crafts into the world of art. Goldsmiths and jewelers created beautiful earrings, nose rings, necklaces, armbands, leg and ankle bands, and other adornments. Architects carved cave temples into the mountainsides

Indian goldsmiths made beautiful jewelry and ornamental objects such as this small gold bull.

and built ornate temple towers that reached to the heavens. Kings, Brahmans, and nobles devoted themselves to the fine arts of sculpture and painting.

Indian sculptors worked in a variety of materials, including wood, ivory, clay, bronze, and stone. They created small figurines and towering statues. They covered pillars, palaces, shrines, and temples with an incredible variety of carved designs. Most sculpture was inspired by religion. A single wall panel might bear images of nature spirits, the Hindu gods and goddesses, and scenes from the life of the Buddha. At the same time, sculptors vividly portrayed the world around them. Their earthy images of nature and human life reflected the Hindu belief that all things, from flowers to men to mountaintops, are part of the One God.

Ancient India's painters created everything from small portraits to giant murals, which decorated the walls of temples, palaces, and grand estates. Few of these early paintings have survived. The finest remaining examples are the murals discovered in thirty caves near the Indian village of Ajanta. The Ajanta caves served as Buddhist temples and monasteries in ancient times. They are decorated with illustrations of Buddhist legends. These wall paintings portray a world teeming with handsome princes and jeweled court ladies, beggars and holy men, gods and demons, birds and animals. Although the Ajanta cave paintings have deteriorated over the centuries, they are still full of color, movement, and life.

Religious paintings and sculptures served a practical purpose. They helped explain the complicated concepts of Hinduism and Buddhism to worshippers who could not read. The creation of religious art also was considered a form of worship. An artists'

Ancient India's sculptors created wondrous scenes in stone. At the center of this stone relief is the life-giving Ganges River.

Abodes of the Gods

One of the largest concentrations of Hindu temples is found at Bhubaneswar, near the east coast of India. Beginning in the third century B.C., thousands of shrines were built at this sacred site. About five hundred still survive. Nearly every surface of these soaring temple towers is crowded with elaborate carvings. Monkeys play and lions roar. Men and women make love in flowering gardens. The gods and goddesses are revealed in all their glory. "At all places where the eye rests," wrote the modern Indian poet Rabindranath Tagore, "the busy chisel of the artist has worked incessantly. The abode of god has been enveloped by a variety of figures depicting the good and the evil, the great as well as the insignificant, the daily occurrences of human life."

manual written during the Gupta Empire called painting "the best of all arts" because it contributed to the fulfillment of the painter's dharma (moral duty) and led to spiritual liberation. "Painting cleanses the mind and curbs anxiety," said the text, "augments [adds to] future good, causes the greatest delight, kills the evils of bad dreams and pleases the household deity."

Chapter VI

OUTCASTES AND SLAVES

The lowest segment of Indian society were the outcastes, often known in modern times as untouchables. Because they did not belong to one of the four chief castes, these "low-born" men and women were not considered members of society at all.

The outcastes worked at trades that were condemned in the religious texts because the work involved taking life or performing other "impure" tasks. Outcastes swept the streets and disposed of garbage and human waste. They worked as hunters, fishermen, butchers, executioners, and grave diggers. Even the leatherworker who made sandals for the king was despised, because he worked with the hides of dead animals. According to the *Laws of Manu*, the gods had "created animals for the sake of sacrifices." A person who killed an animal or handled its remains for any purpose besides religious rituals was contaminated and would "suffer a violent death in future births."

The Untouchables

Ancient Indian texts contain few references to the outcastes. However, it is clear that these despised people nearly always lived in poverty and humiliation.

Outcastes had to live outside the towns and cities, in isolated quarters or villages. They were forbidden to enter a temple or

Beloved Beasts

The ancient Indians loved and respected all animals. Even a bird or an insect might contain the reborn soul of a friend or ancestor. The most revered animals were cattle. Cows were believed to be a gift from the gods because they provided five essential products, milk, curds, butter, urine (used in medicines), and dung (used as fuel). Bulls were associated with the Hindu god Shiva, who rode the sacred white bull Nandi. Many coins, seals, and small clay figures bore images of bulls. So did monumental carvings topping the pillars erected by kings. Indian sculptors also created magnificent stone and metal statues of Nandi to watch over the temples of Shiva.

An Indian woman shows her devotion to Nandi, sacred bull of the Hindu god Shiva.

drink from a public well. In some time periods, they could not use the public roads. According to the sacred laws, they were supposed to eat from cracked bowls and wear clothing that had been stripped from the dead.

Most importantly, outcastes had to be careful not to spread their spiritual pollution. People of higher birth could be defiled by even the sight of one of these condemned individuals. The Chinese traveler Faxian observed that outcastes entering a marketplace would "strike a piece of wood to make themselves known, so that men know and avoid them." Those who accidentally came into contact with an untouchable could purify themselves through various rituals. One religious text advised them to bathe their eyes with perfumed water and avoid food and drink for the rest of the day.

Foreigners living in India, known as *mleccha*, or "jabberers," were also considered outcastes. A man of caste could not share a meal or take part in a variety of other social customs with a *mleccha*. However, foreigners were not subjected to the same discrimination as the untouchables. A monk, scholar, or ambassador visiting from a foreign land was treated with the respect due to his rank. Ancient records show that some long-term visitors were even initiated into a caste, becoming full-fledged members of Indian society.

The Lives of Slaves

"All Indians are free," observed Megasthenes, "and not one of them is a slave." Modern-day historians believe that the ancient Greek scholar was wrong. The Indians did own slaves. However, slavery was much less widespread and severe in India than in many other ancient civilizations.

India's slaves included foreign prisoners captured in war, criminals sentenced to a period of labor for their crimes, and debtors

A Female Militia

Young Greek women who were imported into India as slaves were especially prized in the royal palace. Some slaves became wives or servants in the king's harem. Others joined the harem guard. The *Ramayana* called the members of this female militia "the flower of womanhood." Ancient paintings and sculptures often show the women standing before the harem doors, wearing helmets and armed with long spears.

who could not pay the money they had borrowed. In times of famine, a man might sell his children into slavery to save them from starving. Slaves could be bought and sold, given as gifts, and passed on as part of an inheritance. Children born to a slave automatically belonged to their mother's master.

Most slaves worked as servants in the homes of wealthy families. The laws were designed to protect them from cruel treatment. The *Arthasastra* imposed hefty fines for "deceiving a slave of his money . . . employing a slave to carry the dead . . . or hurting or abusing him or her. . . . Violence towards an attendant of high birth shall entitle him to run away." In some ways, slaves were better off than the wage-earning Sudras. If they became too sick or too old to work, their owners were required to support them. A master also had to pay the funeral expenses for a slave who died in his service.

There were several ways for slaves to recover their freedom. Prisoners of war could pay a ransom, either with money or a period of labor, usually one year. Convicted criminals were freed after they had served their term. Debtors could work off their

Most slaves served wealthy families. This mural from the Ajanta caves shows slaves holding parasols (umbrellas) to protect their masters from the sun.

debts. Slaves also could buy their freedom with money earned in their spare time, or their relatives could redeem them.

A special ceremony marked the release of an Indian man from slavery. Reciting a sacred formula, a priest washed the man's forehead with water from a pitcher, which was then broken into pieces. Purified by this ritual, the man once again took his place in society.

Chapter VII

POETS AND PLAYWRIGHTS

The ancient Indians left behind a wide variety of writings spanning more than two thousand years. Some literature was sacred, believed to have been inspired by the gods. The earliest sacred Hindu texts were the Vedas, which were first compiled sometime around 1500 B.C. A number of later commentaries explored and expanded on the Vedic scriptures. The most important of these commentaries were the Upanishads, a collection of philosophical writings on the meaning of life and the nature of the universe.

India's secular (nonreligious) literature included poetry, drama, and collections of short stories and fables. Ancient writers also produced texts on government, science, and other worldly subjects. Some of the finest secular literature came from the golden age of the Gupta Empire. The Gupta rulers were great supporters of the arts, including the art of writing.

Most writers came from the upper classes. Kings, Brahmans, and nobles were especially fond of writing plays and poetry. The importance of literature in the life of the cultured gentleman was summed up in a proverb. "The man who knows nothing of literature, music or art is nothing but a beast without the beast's tail and horns."

A Refined Language

Most ancient Indian literature was written in **Sanskrit,** which was the strict and formal language of the upper classes. Sanskrit was written down in several different alphabets. Each had its own set of symbols, or **characters,** to represent the letters.

The common people spoke a variety of less complex dialects, or regional languages. Most Buddhist texts were written in a dialect called Pali. By using the language of the ordinary people, the Buddhists hoped to spread their teachings to the masses.

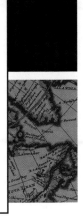

The Pleasures of Poetry

Ancient India's secular poets wrote chiefly about love, nature, morality, and the exploits of kings. They delighted in ornate language and clever wordplay. One Sanskrit poet wrote an entire poem without any "s" sounds to please a young prince who had a speech impediment. Another poet composed a poem that had one meaning when it was read from left to right and a completely different sense when read from right to left. Single-verse poems were very popular. Many of these verses were collected and preserved in anthologies.

In Gupta times, kings and princes often held literary competitions for the most gifted writers. The host presented a theme. Then the contestants took turns showing off their talents. They might compose riddles or puns, act out a charade, or recite a poem on the subject. A panel of judges chose the winner, who was awarded the title "master of knowledge." According to ancient texts, the competition for this honor could be fierce. Some poets were even known to slip bribes to the judges to guarantee victory.

Ancient India's best-known poet was Kalidasa, who is believed to have lived in the fifth century A.D. Only a few of his poems have survived. "The Cloud Messenger" tells the tale of a god who is separated from his wife and decides to send her a message through a passing rain cloud. The lover describes the path the cloud will take over farms, cities, rivers like "a single strand of pearls," and mountains "as white as a freshly cut piece of ivory." Kalidasa's fine depictions of nature and deep human emotions have made "The Cloud Messenger" one of India's most popular Sanskrit poems.

Most of ancient India's surviving poetry was written by men. However, some women also wrote folk songs, hymns, and poetry. The earliest known anthology of women's literature was the *Therigatha,* a collection of **lyric poetry** by Buddhist nuns. Composed in the sixth century B.C., around the time of the Buddha, the songs proclaimed the transforming power of the wise man's teachings. A nun named Mutta celebrated her escape from kitchen drudgery and an unhappy marriage into enlightenment.

> So free am I, so gloriously free,
> Free from three petty things—
> From **mortar,** from **pestle** and from my twisted lord,
> Freed from rebirth and death I am,
> And all that has held me down
> Is hurled away.

Dramatic Traditions

Ancient Indian drama probably began with public performances of sacred legends during religious festivals. By Gupta times, drama was mainly reserved for the upper classes. India had no public theaters. Instead, plays were performed in temples,

Two Great Epics

India's earliest secular literature is found in the *Mahabharata* and the *Ramayana*. The *Mahabharata* is the older of these two epic poems. Composed during the Vedic Period, it was handed down orally for centuries before it was first written down around 500 B.C.

The *Ramayana* tells the story of a heroic king who destroys a powerful demon to rescue his devoted wife. The *Mahabharata* is the tale of a great civil war. Comprised of nearly 100,000 **stanzas,** it may be the world's longest poem. Its most famous segment is the *Bhagavad Gita*, a sermon from the god Krishna. Urging a warrior to fulfill his dharma by fighting a "righteous battle," the god proclaims, "There is more joy in doing one's own duty badly than in doing another man's duty well."

The central event of the *Mahabharata* is a great battle involving a host of gods and heroes.

The Code of the Dance

In ancient India, dancing was closely connected with acting. Dancers used an elaborate code of steps, facial expressions, and gestures to tell a story. Every tilt of the head, twitch of the brow, and movement of a finger had a meaning. One ancient text describes more than one hundred different positions of the head, neck, eyes, hands, and body. These poses could indicate not only emotions but also creatures and objects such as an animal, a flower, or a god.

Many ancient paintings and sculptures captured the expressive code of the dance. Archaeologists have found temples crowded with statues of dancers performing for the gods. Some of the figures demonstrate steps and gestures still used today by traditional dancers in India.

A stone relief captures one of the expressive poses of traditional Indian dance.

palaces, and the homes of the wealthy. They were usually staged during celebrations such as festivals and weddings.

The performers in Indian plays were professional actors. These men and women usually came from the lower classes, and they were often condemned for their loose morals. One ancient text claimed that a man asking an actress the question "Whose are you?" would always get the same answer, "I am yours." Despite their scandalous reputation, especially beautiful actresses and talented actors could gain considerable fame and fortune.

Indian dramas ranged from short one-act plays to long productions with ten or more acts. Many plays were based on tales of the gods and legendary heroes. There were also historical dramas, comedies about life in the royal harem, and morality tales, in which each character represented a particular vice or virtue.

Regardless of their length or subject, all plays followed certain rules and traditions. There were a number of "stock" characters, such as the noble hero, the loyal wife, the evil villain, and the hero's comical but true-blue best friend. The audience could instantly tell what types of characters the actors were playing by their elaborate costumes, as well as their language. Upper-class characters spoke Sanskrit. Lower-ranking characters and most of the female parts spoke one of the dialects.

Plays were performed with few props and no scenery. The actors used words, gestures, and dancing to tell the story. They often expressed a wide range of emotions, from love, joy, and pride to fear, sorrow, anger, and loathing. Even plays with tragic scenes always had a happy ending. The goal of the playwright was to take the audience through a series of different emotions to a state of peace and delight.

Ancient India's greatest poet was also its finest playwright. Kalidasa probably wrote a number of plays, but only three have survived. His masterpiece was *Sakuntala.* This fairy-tale romance was based on a story from the epic *Mahabharata.* Sakuntala, the beautiful daughter of a heavenly nymph, marries the virtuous king Dushyanta. Bewitched by a curse, Dushyanta forgets his wife. Abandoned and heartbroken, Sakuntala returns to heaven, lamenting her fate. Finally, a magic ring restores the king's memory. Visiting the lower slopes of heaven, he sees a small boy playing with a lion cub and realizes that the "little warrior" is his son. The lovers are reunited, and "by the will of heaven," they all live happily ever after.

Chapter VIII

THE LEGACY OF ANCIENT INDIA

Following the fall of the Gupta Empire around A.D. 550, India divided into a multitude of warring kingdoms. In later centuries, the land was dominated by a series of foreign rulers. These included Muslim conquerors from the Arabian Peninsula, the **Mongols,** the Mughals (a Muslim empire of Turkish and Mongol origin), and the British. In 1947, India became an independent, democratic republic.

Today, India's culture is a rich blend of old and new, native and foreign. While its society has been molded by centuries of invasion, migration, and other contacts with the outside world, much of the ancient way of life has survived. Most Indians still live in farming villages. The teachings of Hinduism continue to govern the way they work, dress, eat, marry, raise their children, and worship their gods. In large cities, merchants in small open shops sell spices, incense, flower garlands, and other traditional goods in the shadow of modern office buildings and soaring skyscrapers. Every year, millions of pilgrims visit Hindu shrines and other holy sites. Every day,

Brahman priests recite Vedic hymns that were composed more than three thousand years ago.

The legacy of ancient India also lives on in lands far from its shores. India was one of the birthplaces of civilization, and over time, elements of its culture spread across the globe. Some of its contributions to our modern world include Arabic numerals, algebra, trigonometry, calculus, the decimal system, chess, and the martial arts. Today, people from many lands enjoy the beauty of ancient Indian craftwork, paintings, and sculptures. The ancient

Many traditions and rituals from ancient times are still practiced in India today.

Speaking Sanskrit

As the culture of ancient India spread across the globe, many Indian words found their way into the languages of other lands. Here are a few of the dozens of English words derived from Hindi, a dialect of northern India, and from Sanskrit, the literary language of the ancient Hindus: *bangle, brilliant, candy, cheetah, cot, crimson, ginger, guru, hemp, indigo, jungle, lacquer, loot, musk, navigation, opal, orange, pepper, punch, shampoo, sugar, yoga.*

tales of gods, kings, and heroes have found new life in novels, comic books, TV programs, and movies in many different languages.

India's greatest impact on global culture has been in the fields of philosophy and religion. The influence of Buddhism has been especially widespread. While the Buddhist religion largely died out in India, it became a dominant faith in China, Korea, Japan, and many other Asian nations. In recent decades, Hindu and Buddhist traditions of spirituality, meditation, and yoga have also made a growing impression in the Western world.

Today, millions of tourists travel to India each year to visit early Buddhist shrines and Hindu temples. Touring ancient monuments and enjoying modern-day celebrations of age-old festivals, they witness the lasting glories of India's brilliant civilizations. This ancient land's enduring legacy is captured in an inscription in the Ajanta caves. "A man continues to enjoy himself in paradise as long as his memory is green in the world. One should therefore set up a memorial . . . that will endure for as long as the sun and moon continue."

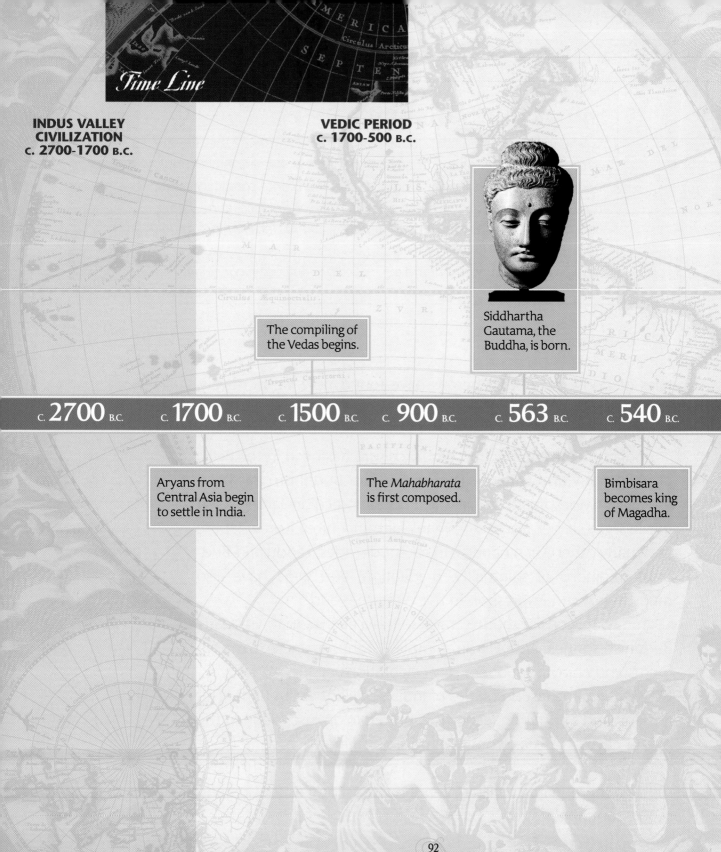

Time Line

INDUS VALLEY CIVILIZATION
c. 2700-1700 B.C.

VEDIC PERIOD
c. 1700-500 B.C.

The compiling of the Vedas begins.

Siddhartha Gautama, the Buddha, is born.

| c. **2700** B.C. | c. **1700** B.C. | c. **1500** B.C. | c. **900** B.C. | c. **563** B.C. | c. **540** B.C. |

Aryans from Central Asia begin to settle in India.

The *Mahabharata* is first composed.

Bimbisara becomes king of Magadha.

AGE OF EMPIRES
C. 500 B.C.-A.D. 550

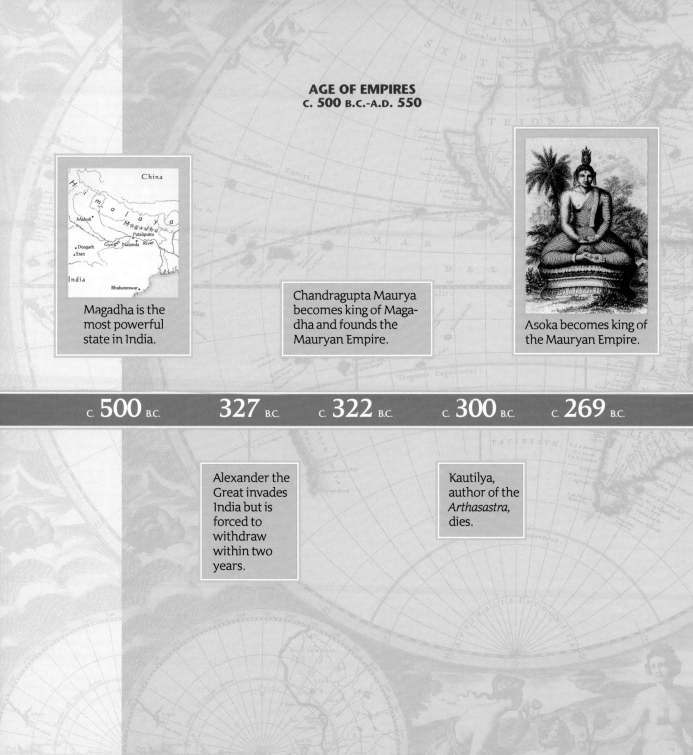

Magadha is the most powerful state in India.

Chandragupta Maurya becomes king of Magadha and founds the Mauryan Empire.

Asoka becomes king of the Mauryan Empire.

c. **500** B.C.	**327** B.C.	c. **322** B.C.	c. **300** B.C.	c. **269** B.C.

Alexander the Great invades India but is forced to withdraw within two years.

Kautilya, author of the *Arthasastra*, dies.

AGE OF EMPIRES
c. 500 B.C.–A.D. 550

Asoka dies, and the Mauryan Empire begins to decline.

The sacred caste laws are set down in the *Laws of Manu*.

Samudra Gupta becomes king of the Gupta Empire.

| c. 261 B.C. | c. 232 B.C. | c. A.D. 150 | c. A.D. 200 | c. A.D. 320 | c. A.D. 335 |

Asoka conquers the eastern kingdom of Kalinga.

Rudradaman repairs a huge dam in Junagadh.

Chandra Gupta I founds the Gupta Empire.

AGE OF EMPIRES
c. 500 B.C.-A.D. 550

Chandra Gupta II becomes king of the Gupta Empire.

The White Huns invade again, overrunning western India.

Some Gupta kings rule locally, but the great empire has ended.

c. A.D. **380**	c. A.D. **453**	c. A.D. **495**	c. A.D. **499**	c. A.D. **550**

India halts an invasion by the White Huns.

Aryabhata writes the scientific text known as the *Aryabhatiya*.

Aryabhata (ar-YBUT-uh)

A.D. 476-550

The scientist and mathematician Aryabhata wrote the *Aryabhatiya,* a text summing up ancient India's knowledge of astronomy and mathematics. The mathematical part of his text covered arithmetic, algebra, trigonometry, and other advanced concepts. The astronomical section contained remarkably accurate observations of the solar system and correctly explained the causes of eclipses of the sun and moon.

Asoka (uh-SHOW-kuh)

Ruled c. 269-232 B.C.

Asoka was the grandson of Chandragupta Maurya and one of the greatest kings of the Mauryan Empire. Early in his reign, he expanded the domain through the brutal conquest of Kalinga, a powerful kingdom on the east coast of India. After this victory, he converted to Buddhism and devoted himself to spreading that faith's beliefs and practices. Asoka sent Buddhist missionaries to every country in the known world and appointed special government officials to ensure the well-being of his subjects.

Bimbisara

Ruled c. 540-490 B.C.

Bimbisara took the throne of Magadha, a kingdom in northeast India, at age fifteen. He was a skilled political and military leader who expanded his domain through conquests and marriage alliances, laying the foundations for the Mauryan Empire. Bimbisara lived at the same time as the Buddha and was an early supporter of Buddhism.

Chandragupta Maurya (chun-druh-GOOP-tuh MOW-ur-yuh)

Ruled c. 322-298 B.C.

Chandragupta was the founder of the Mauryan Empire. The son of a low-caste farmer, he assembled an army of peasants and mercenaries and seized the throne of Magadha around 322 B.C. He went on to conquer all but the southern tip of the Indian peninsula. As king, he established a highly efficient administrative system that became the model for later governments.

Chandra Gupta I

Ruled c. A.D. 320-335

Chandra Gupta I founded the Gupta Empire. The son of a minor ruler, he built a large empire in northern India through conquests and alliances. After ruling for about fifteen years, Chandra Gupta chose his most capable son, Samudra Gupta, as his successor.

Chandra Gupta II

Ruled c. A.D. 380-413

Chandra Gupta II was the son of Samudra Gupta and the third king of the Gupta Empire. He inherited a vast domain and extended its borders through conquests and alliances. Much of the information about his reign comes from the accounts of the Chinese Buddhist monk Faxian.

Kalidasa (kah-lih-DAH-suh)

Fifth century A.D.

Kalidasa was a Sanskrit poet and dramatist who is believed to have lived during the reign of Chandra Gupta II. His surviving poetry consists mainly of two epic poems and two short poems, including "The Cloud Messenger." The most famous of his three surviving plays is the romantic drama *Sakuntala*.

Kautilya (kow-TEEL-yuh)

Died c. 300 B.C.

A Brahman philosopher and statesman, Kautilya is believed to have served as prime minister to Chandragupta Maurya. He wrote the famous political manual the *Arthasastra* ("Science of Material Gain"). This handbook on the theories and principles of government is one of the most important sources of information on the Mauryan Empire.

Mutta (MOO-tuh)

Sixth century B.C.

Mutta was a Buddhist nun whose poetry appeared in the ancient anthology *Therigatha.* According to a commentary accompanying the anthology, she was the daughter of a poor Brahman from the region of Kosala. After Mutta was given in marriage to a hunchbacked Brahman, she persuaded her husband to let her renounce the world and join a community of nuns. Her poems celebrate her release from her unhappy marriage and the joys of achieving spiritual enlightenment.

Rudradaman

Ruled c. A.D. 130-155

King Rudradaman belonged to the Shakas, a powerful ruling family that invaded India from Iran during the period between the Mauryan and Gupta empires. A rock inscription at Junagadh in northwest India describes his military victories and his rebuilding of a huge dam that had been constructed centuries earlier by Chandragupta Maurya.

Samudra Gupta

Ruled c. A.D. 335-380

Samudra Gupta was the second king of the Gupta Empire. He was a great military leader whose many conquests expanded the kingdom to include most of present-day India. He was also a patron of the arts and an accomplished poet and musician. Much of his history is known through the coins he issued and through an inscription on a pillar at Allahabad.

Siddhartha Gautama (sih-DAR-tuh GOW-tuh-muh)

c. 563-483 B.C.

Siddhartha Gautama was the Indian prince who founded the Buddhist religion. He is usually known as the Buddha, or "Enlightened One." Siddhartha was born to a noble family but gave up his wealth and privileges in a quest for spiritual peace. After years of wandering and self-denial, he achieved enlightenment. For the rest of his life, he traveled from place to place, preaching to his disciples. After his death, his followers wrote down his teachings and carried Buddhism to many different lands.

archaeologists   scientists who study the physical remains of past cultures to learn about human life and activity

arsenal   a place where weapons are made and stored

astrologers   persons who predict human affairs based on the supposed influence of the stars and planets

astronomy   the scientific study of the sun, moon, stars, and other heavenly bodies

Brahmans   the top caste in Indian society, traditionally made up of priests

Buddhist   relating to Buddhism, the religion based on the teachings of the fifth-century B.C. Indian wise man Siddhartha Gautama, known as the Buddha, or "Enlightened One"

bureaucracy   a complex government system with many levels of departments and officials

caravans   groups of people and pack animals traveling together, often through a desert or other dangerous land

carbon dating   a scientific method used to date ancient objects by measuring the amount of the atom carbon 14 in the object. The method is also known as radiocarbon dating.

castes   the Western term for the Indian class system

characters   symbols used in writing

chaturanga   an ancient Indian board game that is believed to be the earliest form of chess

concubines   the secondary wives of a king or other high-ranking man. Concubines had lower status and fewer rights than the principal wife.

crown prince   the male next in line to the throne, usually the king's oldest son

curds   thickened clumps of milk

curry a mixture of strongly flavored spices used to season foods

deciphered decoded or interpreted

deity a god or goddess

dharma (DAR-muh) in Hinduism, the duties that are divinely assigned to each individual as a result of his or her birth into a particular caste

dhoti (DOH-tee) a garment worn by Indian men and women, made of a length of cloth about 6 to 9 yards (5.5 to 8 meters) long, which is wrapped around the lower body and tied at the waist

domesticated animals trained or adapted to live close to people and to be useful to them

edicts official public announcements of policies and laws

enlightenment in Buddhism, the blissful state of total knowledge and freedom from desire

epic a long narrative poem telling the story of historical or legendary heroes

guru (GOO-roo) an Indian religious teacher and spiritual guide

harem a special secluded section in an ancient Indian royal palace, where the king's wives and daughters lived

Hinduism the dominant religion of India, which is one of the oldest world religions still practiced today. Hinduism is a flexible faith with a wide variety of scriptures, beliefs, and practices.

inscriptions words written or engraved on stone, metal, or another hard surface

Jainism a religion founded in India in the sixth century B.C., which teaches that salvation can be achieved through a life of complete nonviolence, meditation, fasting, and other forms of strict self-denial

jatis (JAH-teez) subgroups within the four main Hindu classes, based mainly on family descent and occupation

karma in Hinduism and Buddhism, the total effect of a person's actions during his or her present and previous lives, which determines the person's destiny

Kshatriyas (kshuh-TREE-uhs)   the second class in Indian society, traditionally made up of warriors and government leaders

lyric poetry   short songlike poems expressing deep personal emotions

moksha   (MAWK-shuh)   in Hinduism, the highest stage of religious awareness, in which a person is liberated from the cycle of death and rebirth and achieves supreme knowledge and bliss

monasteries   places where monks (men who belong to a religious order) live and work apart from the world

Mongols   nomadic peoples from Mongolia, north of China, who created the world's largest land empire in the thirteenth century A.D.

mortar   a sturdy bowl in which seeds, grains, and other substances are crushed or mashed with a pestle

nomads   groups of people who wander from place to place, often with herds of grazing livestock

panas   coins commonly used in ancient India, made mainly out of silver

pestle   a club-shaped utensil for crushing and mashing substances in a mortar

puja   a Hindu ritual in which the worshipper demonstrates his or her devotion to a god by offering food, flowers, prayers, songs, dancing, and other gifts and attentions to an image believed to contain the god's spirit

pyre   a pile of flammable materials for burning a dead body as part of a funeral rite

reincarnation   the rebirth of the soul after death into a new body. The belief in reincarnation is central to Hinduism, Buddhism, Jainism, and many other religions.

sacrament   a religious ritual

Sanskrit   the literary language of the upper classes in ancient India

sari   (SAHR-ee)   a garment worn by Indian women, made of a long cloth wrapped around the lower body, with one end either draped over a shoulder or wrapped around the upper body

sati   (seh-TEE)   an ancient Indian practice in which a widow burned herself to death on her husband's funeral pyre as a demonstration of her devotion to him. The word can also refer to the woman who performed the self-sacrifice.

siege the surrounding of a fort or city, during which the attackers cut off food and other supplies to force the enemy to surrender

srenis ancient Indian trade guilds. The *srenis* regulated business practices within their trade and served as banks and courts of law for members.

stanzas the divisions of a poem, made up of two or more lines that rhyme or go together in some other way

stupas (STOO-puhs) dome-shaped buildings that serve as Buddhist shrines

Sudras (SOO-druhs) the lowest caste in Indian society, traditionally made up of servants, laborers, and craftspeople

turban a headdress worn by Indian men and sometimes women, made from a length of fabric wrapped around the head

untouchables the people at the lowest level of Indian society, who were regarded as "outcastes" not worthy of a place within the social order. In ancient times, it was believed that a person of higher birth was contaminated by contact with an untouchable.

Vaishyas (VYSH-yuhs) the third class in Indian society, traditionally made up of farmers and merchants

varnas the four great social classes of Indian society

Vedas (VAY-duhs) ancient collections of religious poems, hymns, and sacrificial formulas that are the earliest sacred literature of Hinduism. The Vedas consist mainly of four books, the *Rig-Veda,* the *Sama-Veda,* the *Yajur-Veda,* and the *Atharva-Veda.*

vina (VEE-nuh) an ancient stringed instrument resembling a small harp, which was played with a bow

whey (WAY) the thin watery liquid that is left after milk is separated and the thick part, or curds, is removed

Books

Hinds, Kathryn. *India's Gupta Dynasty.* Cultures of the Past series. New York: Marshall Cavendish, 1996.

Kirkpatrick, Naida. *The Indus Valley.* Understanding People in the Past series. Chicago: Heinemann, 2002.

Shuter, Jane. *The Indus Valley*. History Opens Windows series. Chicago: Heinemann Library, 2003.

Stewart, Melissa. *Science in Ancient India.* Science of the Past series. New York: Franklin Watts, 1999.

Swan, Erin Pembrey. *India.* Enchantment of the World series. New York: Children's Press, 2002.

Organizations and Online Sites

Ancient India
http://www.ancientindia.co.uk

Explore the history, geography, culture, and beliefs of ancient India through stories, photos, maps, animations, and interactive games. This excellent site is presented by the British Museum.

The Ancient Indus Valley
http://www.harappa.com/har/har0.html

This Web site offers a wealth of information on the archaeology of the Indus Valley civilization, presented by the Harappa Archaeological Research Project. There are links to hundreds of articles plus slide tours of ancient cities.

Birmingham Museum of Art
2000 Eighth Avenue North
Birmingham, AL 35203
http://www.artsbma.org/asart.htm

The Indian gallery in the Birmingham Museum's Asian Art Collection includes fine examples of Buddhist and Hindu sculptures. Visit the Web site for photos and descriptions of selected items.

Daily Life in Ancient India
http://members.aol.com/Donnclass/Indialife.html

This "kid friendly" site provides lots of information about homes, food, clothing, jobs, sports, games, and other aspects of daily life in India from 3000 B.C. to A.D. 700.

History for Kids: Ancient India
http://www.historyforkids.org/learn/india/

This easy-to-read site offers information on ancient India's history, environment, religion, society, food, clothing, science, art, and architecture.

Los Angeles County Museum of Art
5909 Wilshire Boulevard
Los Angeles, CA 90036
http://www.lacma.org

Nearly half of the museum's extensive collection of artwork from India through the centuries is available online. You can use the site's search engine to locate items of special interest. For example, you might search for artifacts from a particular time period or for a specific category such as "elephant" or "Vishnu."

The Metropolitan Museum of Art
1000 Fifth Avenue
New York, NY 10028-0198
http://www.metmuseum.org/works_of_art

The Metropolitan Museum has the largest collection of Asian art in the Western world. Its Web site offers photos and descriptions of fifty items from the collection, including examples of ancient Indian sculpture and jewelry.

The Norton Simon Museum of Art
411 West Colorado Boulevard
Pasadena, CA 91105
http://www.nortonsimon.org/collections/

The Norton Simon Museum's collection of South Asian art includes religious sculptures and engraved columns, pillars, and other architectural features. Visit the Web site for photos and descriptions.

The Ramayana: An Enduring Tradition
http://www.maxwell.syr.edu/maxpages/special/ramayana/

Designed by teachers participating in a summer study program, this site explores the epic poem the *Ramayana.* There are summaries of the story, traditional paintings, photographs of modern performances, and articles on Hindu beliefs and gods.

Seattle Art Museum
100 University Street
Seattle, WA 98101
http://www.seattleartmuseum.org/Teach/learnOnline.asp

The Seattle Art Museum's South and Southeast Asian Collection includes Buddhist and Hindu sculpture, paintings, and decorative arts. Visit the "Learn Online" page for a variety of interactive games with terrific art and music.

Index

Actors, 87
Afghanistan, 5
Agni (god), 14
Ajanta caves, 74, *81*, 91
Alexander the Great, 39
Arabic numerals, 41, 90
Archaeology
    carbon dating, 67
    coins, 24, *24*, 61
    excavations, 5, 9, *9*, 12, 22, 29, *54*, 64, 86
    Mehrgarh settlement, 54, *54*
    modern customs and, 12
    Pataliputra palace, 29
    yoga and, 45
Art
    Brahmans and, 74
    carvings, *25*, 76
    goldsmiths, 73, *73*
    Gupta Empire, 8, 74, 76
    jewelry, 5, 73
    kings and, 73–74
    paintings, 22, 74, 90
    pottery, 5, 70, *70*
    religion and, 74, 76
    sculpture, 5, *23*, 36, *52*, *73*, 74, *75*, 78, 90
    stone reliefs, *13*, *19*, *26*, *43*, 86
Arthasastra (political handbook), 23, 25, 34–35, 37, 47, 53, 59, 63, 80
Aryabhata (astronomer), 41
Aryan nomads, 6
Asoka (king), 8, 25, 28
Astrology, 33
Astronomy, 41

Basket makers, 71
Bathhouses, 58
Beauty spots, 31
Bhagavad Gita (poem), 14, 85
Bhubaneswar temple, 76

Bihar, 40
Bimbisara (king), 6
Blacksmithing, *68*, 69, *69*
Boys, 39–40, 55, 65
Brahma (One God), 13, *13*, 14, 15
Brahman priests, 11, 12, 16, 18, *19*, 21, 27, 34, 35, 39, 40, 50, 66, 74
Buddha, 26, *26*, 27, *27*, 38
Buddhism, 11, 12
    Ajanta caves, 74, *81*, 91
    art and, 74
    Brahman caste and, 21
    Buddha, 26, *26*, 27, *27*, 38
    caste system and, 26
    Eightfold Noble Path, 26
    enlightenment, 26, *28*
    Jatakas (ancient tales), 64
    kings and, 8, 26, 27, 28
    monasteries, 8, 40
    nirvana, 26
    Pali dialect and, 83
    stupas (memorial shrines), 27, *43*
    trade and, 62
    Western expansion of, 91
    "Wheel of Law," *28*
Bureaucracy, 35

Caravans, 63–64, *63*
Carbon dating, 67
Carpenters, 68, 72
Carvings, *25*, 76
Caste system. *See also* Brahmas; Kshatriyas; Outcastes; Sudras; Vaishyas.
    Buddhism and, 26
    employment and, 21
    food and, 17, 47
    Hinduism and, 15–17
    jatis (subgroups), 16–17, 72
    marriage and, 17–18
    spiritual purity and, 17

untouchables, 16, 77
  Vedas and, 18
Cattle, 78, *78*
Cavalry, 37, 38
Chandra Gupta I (king), 8
Chandra Gupta II (king), 69
Chandragupta Maurya (king), 23, 25, 37
Chariots, 38–39
Chaturanga (game), 44, *44*
Chess, 44, 90
Chowdhary, Sooryakant Narasinh, 27
Cities
  administration of, 35
  excavations of, 5
  Harappa, 6, *59*
  houses, 6
  Kusinagara, 38
  Maholi, 36
  market districts, 57, 58–59, *59*
  Mohenjo-daro, 6
  Nalanda, 40
  port cities, 61
  Sanchi, 38, *38*, 73
  sewage systems, 6
Civil servants, 35
Clothing, 57
"The Cloud Messenger" poem, 84
Coins, 24, *24*, 61
Concubines, 30, 42
Council of ministers, 34–35
Crafts, 66, 67–71
Cremation, 48, *48*
Criminals, 57
Crops, 5, 50, 52, 56
Crown princes, 32–33, *32*
Cunningham, Sir Alexander, 38

Dance, 86, *86*, 90
Deogarh temple, 20
Deserted women, 66–67
Dharma (religious and social duties), 13, 15
Dhoti (clothing), 57
Districts, 35

Dramas, 84, 87–88
Droughts, 56
Dushyanta (king), 88

Education, 40, *41*, 46–47, 55
Eightfold Noble Path, 26
Elephants, 37, *37*
Enlightenment, 26, *28*

Families, 42–43
Farming
  crop rotation, 52
  crops, 5, 50, 52, 56
  droughts, 56
  fallowing, 52
  fertilizer, 52
  flooding, 6, 56
  government and, 53
  irrigation, 23, 53
  kings and, 50
  livestock, 5, 52, *52*, 54, *55*, 56
  Mehrgarh settlement, 54, *54*
  villages, 53, 54, 55
Faxian (Buddhist monk), 8, 40, 79
Flooding, 6, 56
Food, 17, 29, 47, 53
Funeral pyres, 48, *48*

Games, 44, *44*, 90
Ganesh (God), 14
Ganges River, 6, *75*
Garland making, 71, *71*
Gautama, Siddhartha. *See* Buddha.
Girls, 46–47
Goldsmiths, 73, *73*
Goparaja (chieftain), 48
Government
  Arthasastra (political handbook), 23
  bureaucracy, 35
  business operations and, 36, 58–59
  council of ministers, 34–35
  farming and, 53
  Kshatriyas and, 34

magistrates, 35–36
market districts and, 58–59
spies, 25, 36–37, 59
taxes 18, 35, 50, 56, 58–59, 61–62
wages, 37
Great Britain, 89
Great Stupa at Sanchi, 38, *38*, 73
Gupta Empire, 12,*13*, 15, 20, 28, 41, 74,
    82, 89
Gurus, 40, *41*

Harappa, 6, *59*
Harem guards, 80
Harems, 30, *30*, 31, *31*, 36, 80
Harsacarita ("Deeds of Harsa"), 45
Hermitages, 21, 45
Hermits, 39, 45
Himalayan Mountains, 6
Hindi dialect, 91
Hinduism, 89–90, 91
  art and, 74, 76
  Bhubaneswar temple, 76
  Brahma (One God), 13, *13*, 15
  Brahmans (priests), 11, 12
  caste system and, 15–17
  dharma, 13
  gods and goddesses, 14
  Gupta Empire, 12
  gurus, 40
  karma, 13
  kings and, 8
  Laws of Manu (sacred texts), 17
  modern culture and, 89–90
  moksha (liberation), 13
  Nandi (sacred white bull), 78, *78*
  puja ritual, 15
  reincarnation, 12–13
  sacred thread, 39–40, *40*
  Sudra caste and, 65
  temples, 20, 76
  Upanishads (commentaries on the
    Vedas), 13
  Vedas (religious poems), 6, 8–9, 11, 16,

18, *41*, 50, 55, 65, 82, 90
Western expansion of, 91
Horse sacrifice ritual, 24, *24*
Householders, 39, 40, 42, 43, 45

Indus Valley civilization, 5, 6,
    9, 45, *46*, *51*, *59*, *68*, *70*
Indus Valley region, 5
Infantry, *37*, 39
Initiation ceremonies, 39–40, 65
Iron Pillar of Delhi, 69, *69*
Irrigation systems, 23, 53

Jainism, 11
Jatakas (ancient tales), 64
Jatis (class subgroups), 16–17
Jewelry, 5, 73
Junagadh, 35

Kalidasa (poet and playwright), 84, 87–88
Kamasutra ("Rules of Love"), 44–45
Karma (sum of good and bad), 13, 66
Kautilya (chief minister), 23
Kings. *See also* Kshatriya caste.
  art and, 73–74
  astrology and, 33
  Brahmans and, 21
  Buddhism and, 8, 26, 27, 28
  concubines of, 30
  council of ministers and, 35
  crown princes, 32–33
  crowning of, 33
  farm estates of, 50
  food tasters, 29
  harems, 30, *30*, 31, 36
  horse sacrifice ritual, 24
  irrigation projects and, 53
  literary competitions, 83
  palaces, 22, 28–29, 33
  religion and, 23
  responsibilities of, 23, 25
  royal edicts, 8, 9, 22, 25, 35
  sacred duties, 23, 25

selection of, 22, 32
servants of, 29, *29*
spies of, 25
wives of, 30
Kohl (eyeliner), 31, *31*
Krishna (god), 14, 56
Kshatriya caste, 16, 22, 34, 35,
    37, 39, 40, 43, 46–47, 66. *See also*
    Kings.
Kusinagara, 38

Lakshmi (goddess), 14, 43
Language
  Aryan, 6
  Sanskrit, 83, 84, 87, 91
  stone seals, 6
Laws of Manu (sacred texts), 17,
    18, 45, 49, 50, 65, 77
Libby, Willard, 67
Literature
  anthologies, 83
  Bhagavad Gita (poem), 14, 85
  Gupta Empire and, 8, 82
  Jatakas (ancient tales), 64
  literary competitions, 83
  lyric poetry, 84
  Mahabharata (epic poem), 6, 14, 22,
    33, 80, 85, *85*, 88
  poetry, 6, 83–84
  Ramayana (epic poem), 6, 14, 22, 33, 80,
    85
  secular literature, 82
  Therigatha (poetry collection), 84
  Upanishads (commentaries on the Vedas),
    13, 82
  Vedas (religious poems), 6, 8–9, 11, 16,
  18, *41*, 50, 55, 65, 82, 90
The Little Clay Cart (play), 36
Livestock, 5, 52, *52*, 54, *55*, 56
Lyric poetry, 84

Magadha (king), 6
Magistrates, 35–36

Mahabharata (epic poem), 6, 14, 22, 33,
    80, 85, *85*, 88
Maholi, 36
Makeup, 31, *31*
Map, *7*
Market districts, 57, 58–59, *59*
Marriage, 17–18, 40, 42, *42*, 47, 49, *49*
Mathematics, 41, 90
Mauryan Empire, 6, 8, 28, 61
Medicine, 41
Megasthenes (Greek historian),
    25, 36, 53, 62, 79
Mehrgarh settlement, 54, *54*
Merchants, 5–6, 50, *51*, 56–58, 60, *63*
Military
  cavalry, 37, 38
  chariots, 37, 38–39
  elephants, 37, *37*
  infantry, 37, *37*, 39
  Kshatriyas and, 34, 37
  siege of Kusinagara, 38, *38*
Milkmen, 56
Mleccha (foreigners), 79
Mohenjo-daro, 6
Moksha (liberation), 13
Monasteries, 8, 40
Mongols, 89
Mother Goddess, 12, 14, *15*
Mughals, 89
Music, 43–44, *43*
Mutta (Buddhist nun), 84

Nalanda monastery, 40
Nandi (sacred white bull), 78
Nirvana, 26

Oil merchants, 56
Outcastes, 16, 77, 79
Overseers. *See* Spies.

Paintings, 22, 74, 76, 90
Pakistan, 5
Pali dialect, 83

Parvati (goddess), 14
Pataliputra palace, 28–29
Peddlers, 58
Perfumers, 56–57
Plays, 84, 87–88
Pleasure, 43–45
Poetry, 6, 83–84
Potters, 70
Pottery, 5, 70, *70*
Provinces, 35
Puja ritual, 15

Rama (god), 14
Ramayana (epic poem), 6, 14, 22, 33, 80, 85
Reincarnation, 12, 78
Religion. *See* Buddhism; Hinduism.
Rest houses, 62
Rig-Veda (Vedic text), 16
Righteousness, 42
Roads, 35, 62
Royal edicts, 8, 9, 22, 25, 35
Rudradaman (king), 35

Sacred thread, 39–40, *40*
Sakuntala (play), 88
Samudra Gupta, 24
Sanchi, 38, *38*, 73
Sanskrit language, 83, 84, 87, 91
Sarasvati (goddess), 14
Sari (clothing), 57
Sati ("true wife"), 48, *48*
Scales, *51*, 58, *60*
Science, 8, 41
Sculpture, 5, *23*, 36, *52*, 74, *75*, 78, 90
Self-sacrifice, 48, *48*
Shiva (god), 14, 15, *40*, 78
Shoemakers, 72
Silk Road, *63*
Slavery, 56, 79–81, *81*
Spice merchants, 56
Spies, 25, 36–37, 59
Srenis (trade guilds), 71–73

Stone reliefs, *13, 19, 26, 43, 86*
Stone seals, 6, 45, *46*
Street performers, 58
Students, 39
Stupas (memorial shrines), 27, *43*
Sudra caste, 16, 65–71, 80
Surya (god), 14

Tagore, Rabindranath, 76
Taverns, 57, 59
Taxes, 18, 35, 50, 56, 58–59, 61–62
Temples, 20, *20*, 74, 76, 78
Textiles, 71
Theater. *See* Plays.
Therigatha (poetry collection), 84
Tourism, 91
Trade, 50, 61–64, *62, 63*
Turbans, 57

Untouchables, 16, 77, 79
Upanishads (commentaries on the Vedas),
    13, 82

Vaishya caste, 16, 39, 50, 62, 66
Varnas. *See* Castes.
Varuna (god), 14
Vedas (religious poems), 6, 8–9, 11, 16,
    18, *41*, 50, 55, 65, 82, 90
Vedic Period, 6, 85
Vina (musical instrument), 43, *43*
Vishnu (god), 14, 15, 20, *20*, 43

Wanderers, 39, 45–46
War elephants, 37, *37*
Wealth, 43
"Wheel of Law," *28*
White Huns, 8
Women, 66–67, 71

Yama (god), 14
Yoga, 45, *46*

About the Author

Virginia Schomp has written more than fifty titles for young readers on topics including dinosaurs, careers, biographies, and American history. Her writings on cultures of the past include *The Ancient Greeks, Japan in the Days of the Samurai,* and *The Italian Renaissance,* as well as three other titles in the People of the Ancient World series: *The Ancient Chinese, Ancient Mesopotamia,* and *The Vikings.* She is most intrigued by the "story" in history—the writings and remembrances that bring alive the struggles, sorrows, hopes, and dreams of people who lived long ago. Researching the world of ancient India gave her an opportunity to learn more about the faiths and philosophies of Hinduism and Buddhism. It was also fun to rediscover the great epic poem the *Ramayana,* which she first read and enjoyed in comic book form some twenty-five years ago.

Ms. Schomp earned a Bachelor of Arts degree in English Literature from the Pennsylvania State University. She lives in the Catskill Mountain region of New York.